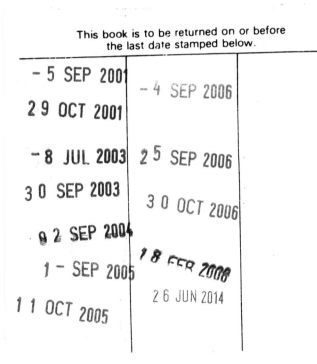

'a man of profound ideals, a man in whose mind stirred the dream of struggle...'

Fidel Castro 1967

332

En Esta Casa
No se reciben otras Prédicas que
no sean las de la REVOLUCION.

CDR
FUNDADOR

VII

David Sandison

'it is then, at the end, that we see the profound tragedy which circumscribes the life of the proletariat the world over'

1952

CHE EVARA

Havana, January 1959

rebel

student

RI X PAN

diplomat

gu

★ ³ revolutionary

★ ⁶ legend

⁵ errilla

The Bolivian government forces who ambushed, overwhelmed and captured a small international band of socialist guerrillas near the remote Andean mountain town of Higueras on October 8, 1967, had every reason to celebrate the success of their mission, especially as they had not found the task too difficult.

Their opponents had been ill-prepared and poorly-armed. Also, and most importantly, many of those who'd been captured and taken into custody were suffering from hunger, fatigue, wounds and a variety of debilitating ailments which combined to make them easy prey for an attack by men who knew the terrain better.

As the soldiers embarked on a long night of triumphant celebratory drinking, their principal satisfaction lay in the fact that one of those wounded in the action, and now securely under lock and key, was none other than Ernesto 'Che' Guevara, the legendary Argentine-born hero of Fidel Castro's outstandingly successful campaign to overthrow the régime of Cuban dictator Fulgencio Batistá in 1959, a man who had subsequently become one of the world's most charismatic and persuasive propagandists for armed revolution in pursuit of international socialism, and the idol of a generation which was even now apparently turning its back on many accepted standards of moral and political behaviour.

If they had only considered the matter more carefully, the security advisers of Bolivian president General René Barrientos would have realized that they had been presented with a unique opportunity to destroy the international personality cult which surrounded their prisoner. Che had come to Bolivia some 11 months earlier with the openly stated mission of persuading the country's ill-used peasants – and especially its poorly-paid, exploited and brutalized tin miners – to support his small brigade's attempt to overthrow Barriento's corrupt, oppressive, US-backed administration.

That mission had, so far, been spectacularly unsuccessful. Local Communist Party leaders and the miners' unions had effectively refused to support Guevara's objectives either physically or politically, preferring the status quo of their harsh existence to the even harsher reality of the government reprisals any such revolt would inevitably bring down upon them and their families. The same was true of the peasants Che and his band encountered, whose natural reserve towards outsiders – let alone armed foreigners dressed in military fatigues – was heightened by a sure knowledge that their presence would bring wrath and retaliation from the Bolivian military.

Although Guevara's band had found some rare pockets of tacit support among the remote villages and townships they visited during those months – especially when it became known that these guerrillas were actually prepared to pay the going rate, and in hard cash, for much-needed supplies – such supplies and foodstuffs invariably ran low during the long periods they were forced to spend deep in the jungle, hiding from the ever-increasing number of government patrols sent in to find and destroy them. Hunger was a constant companion and the idealism of his motley crew had soon been sapped of its initial enthusiasm. Chased and harassed at every turn, Guevara's men may have scored a few

ABOVE Che relaxing with a refreshing bowl of maté.

psychological wins in small skirmishes, but they had enjoyed few real military successes, and certainly no substantial victories.

General Barrientos, therefore, could have scored a major international public relations coup with a show trial of a man whom it would have been easy to portray as a reckless adventurer and, more potently, as an inept loser. Evidence of the overwhelming failure of his Bolivian adventure would have not merely dented Che's image as a modern-day David taking on the Goliath of Yankee imperialism – it could have negated much of his political philosophy as well.

A public trial would also have done much to project an even-handed and responsible image for a régime with a civil rights record that was notorious even by the generally deplorable standards of governments throughout South America.

However, the decision taken by Barrientos the following day – undoubtedly on the advice (or direct orders) of CIA officers based in Bolivia's legislative capital, La Paz – robbed him and his government of what could justifiably be described as a golden opportunity to capitalize on their success.

Instead, they created a martyr whose image and legacy would live on,

far more potent in martyrdom than it may have been had he been allowed to live and face the humiliation of the evidence – that Che had attempted one bold adventure too many, and had continued with that adventure long after it became clear that he lacked the political and physical support of those whose cause he claimed to represent. That decision alone could have been portrayed as wilful and stupid, a stubborn refusal to accept reality and a form of imperialism every bit as arrogant as that practised by Che's sworn enemy, the United States of America.

According to the most reliable reports, Che Guevara – wounded in both legs and unable to walk unaided – had been taken to a schoolhouse in Higueras, along with a number of his comrades. At some stage during the 24 hours in which he and his captors awaited news of his fate, Che refused to answer any questions put to him, but did slap a drunken officer who was taunting him, a defiance typical of a man who abhorred any indiscipline among his own troops and retained a strict sense of dignity, not only of and for himself but in what he expected of others.

When the order to kill Che and his associates arrived from La Paz, the task of carrying it out was given to Mario Terán, a young non-commissioned officer, by the two officers commanding the government detachment, Colonel Andrés Selnich (later to become a general) and Major Miguel Ayoroa.

In his account of Che's murder in his introduction to the first publication of Che's Bolivian campaign diaries, Fidel Castro alleged that Terán was hopelessly drunk. He went to the room where Che lay sprawled on a school bench, alerted by the sound of gunshots which had just despatched two other guerrillas, a Bolivian and a Peruvian. Finding

Guevara awake, Terán hesitated, only to be told: 'Shoot. Don't be afraid.' His nerve gone, Terán fled, but was summarily ordered back by Selnich and Ayoroa. This time he obeyed, aiming his machine-gun fire below Che's waist. According to Castro, this was a ruse to support already-circulating official accounts which claimed that Che had died a few hours after his last battle. His new wounds, therefore, must not be instantly fatal. It was not until a sergeant took pity on him that Che's agonies were ended by a single shot to the heart from beneath his ribs.

Then, in a gruesome and bizarre scenario which would only serve to reinforce his legendary status and create an immense wave of revulsion, outrage and sympathy around the world, he was propped up so that a photographer could immortalize the fallen champion and his victorious captors. Before that happened, Che's face was cosmetically enhanced to bring his battered, emaciated appearance closer to that of the man portrayed in a million posters around the world.

Not included in that infamous line-up was the tall, grim-faced American – generally assumed to be a CIA field operative – who would also hover in the wings some hours later when Che's body was displayed for waiting reporters and photographers in Vallegrande, the nearby provincial capital.

Among those present at Vallegrande was British journalist Richard Gott, then on assignment in Bolivia for the *Manchester Guardian*. Confronted by the media's reluctance to accept their word that this was, indeed, the corpse of Che Guevara – and aware that Gott had met Che in the past – they pressed him into service as a witness. Gott reluctantly confirmed that the wasted, bullet-riddled body laid out in such undignified fashion was that of Ernesto Guevara. Cameras clicked and whirred. The silent American watched grimly.

The final act in this small brutal tragedy was to take place when the reporters were on their way back to La Paz, where they would file the stories which forced news editors around the world to begin re-designing their front pages and re-scheduling radio and TV airtime. A bulldozer which had been employed building a new airfield at Vallegrande was pressed into service, a pit was excavated near the end of the runway site, and the bodies of Che and five of his guerrillas were consigned to a mass grave destined to be covered by cement and tarmac. Before that, Che's hands were cut off, to be sent to a government minister in La Paz who wanted a cast made of them, for use as a gruesome desk ornaments.

In December 1995, following a tip from a Bolivian army officer who'd been present in 1967, several bodies were unearthed, although too decomposed to be properly identified; indeed, they became a matter of some contention between Bolivia and the Cuban government, who wished to have them returned to Havana. Finally, in 1997, a further body was discovered which DNA tests proved positively to be that of Che.

It was a tragic and shoddy end to a relatively short life filled with remarkable, often historically important, incidents. It was a life which continues to fascinate succeeding generations of political commentators, historians and those who still search for heroes prepared to pay the ultimate price in their pursuit of an idealistic cause.

ABOVE The bullet-riddled body of Che Guevara propped up for the whole world's cameras in Vallegrande. Before this macabre event took place, the dead hero's appearance was enhanced to make him more like the Che which looked out from a million posters.

0   2

studer

The Early Years

Ernesto 'Che' Guevara de la Serna was born on 14 June 1928, in Rosario, the most important city in Argentina after the capital, Buenos Aires. He was named after his father, a likeable main-chancer who had made and lost small fortunes in ranching, shipbuilding and growing maté (a tea-like herb drunk either in bitter or sweetened form, most popular in Argentina, Uruguay and Paraguay), before becoming an unqualified and only periodically successful builder-architect.

A noted liberal socialist, Ernesto Sr boasted a distinguished lineage which included Viceroy Liniers, an early Argentine grandee, and Juan Antonio Guevara, who'd been forced to flee into exile in California when he failed to oust the Argentinian dictator Juan Manuel de Rosas in an 1850 uprising. In the lawless Wild West, Juan Antonio had created and led a fearsome gang of rustlers and gold bandits and married a Mexican beauty, Concepción Castro. Their son, who was thus a US citizen by birth, married a woman called Elizabeth Victoria Lynch, from San Lorenzo, California, and it was after the couple quit California and settled in Argentina that Ernesto Guevara Lynch, Che's father, was born.

Che's mother, Celia de la Serna, also came from aristocratic stock, remaining proud of her lineage and pedigree even when her politics changed from liberal socialism to full-blown Marxism. She was, by all accounts, a noted political debater always ready to attack US imperialism in South America and quick to defend those she considered oppressed by Argentina's inevitably corrupt régimes.

Like her husband, Celia permitted and even encouraged her children to let their hearts rule their heads in life decisions. She would offer advice if asked, but was content to let them make their own eventual choices, even though she undoubtedly favoured 'respectable' careers for them all. Also like her husband, Celia loved nothing better than a good argument – the more heated the better – so the various Guevara households often rang with the sound of raised voices.

Those arguments fostered an abiding admiration for both parents in all their children, for they were invariably based on the finer points of political ideology and rarely on such mundane matters as lack of social status or – as could have easily been the case when another of Ernesto Sr's pipe-dreams went up in smoke – the family's often precarious finances.

Che's birthplace was largely accidental. Ernesto and Celia were in Rosario on a business trip concerned with his maté interests when she went into labour a month early and was rushed to hospital. This was the first spectacular manifestation of Che's notorious inability to let matters take their course, a characteristic which would get him into hot water on many future occasions.

The couple's first-born arrived, in his father's words, 'sick and puny', but clearly the apple of both his parents' eyes. This favouritism would continue, especially where his father was concerned, despite the arrival of Che's sister, Celia, two years later, his brother, Roberto (destined to become a prominent lawyer), a year after that, another sister, Ana Maria,

LEFT The future revolutionary and his parents, Ernesto Sr and his beloved mother Celia.

BELOW The Guevara family at play in a public swimming pool. The children are from left, the eight year old Ernesto; sister Celia; sister Ana Maria; and brother Roberto.

in the following year, and the Guevaras' final child, Juan Martin, who was born when Che – nicknamed within his family 'Ernestito' – was 13 years old.

After spending a further 18 months in Misiones Province, Ernesto Sr abandoned his maté estate and moved his young family to the capital, Buenos Aires, to begin a career as a shipbuilder. By now it was clear that his 'puny' son was asthmatic, though not before he had tried to toughen the infant up with cold baths and long sessions of exposure to the elements, whether hot or cold, on the balcony of the family home.

Advised that the humidity of Buenos Aires was not good for Che's condition, Ernesto sold up his partnership interest in the shipyard and relocated his family to the healthier environment of Alta Gracia, a hillside town in Córdoba Province. Ernesto Sr would never rue that decision, even when the shipyard grew to become one of Argentina's biggest and most successful. His son's health and well-being were of far greater importance to him than being a millionaire.

With the profits from his sell-out ensuring that he didn't have to work for some time, Ernesto divided his time between building up a library of 3,000 books and strengthening his weakly son via a régime of swimming, shooting, walking and contact sports, especially rugby and soccer. Swimming played a crucial part in that régime, too, with Che spending up to three hours a day in the family pool during the summer months to help relax his chest and improve his breathing.

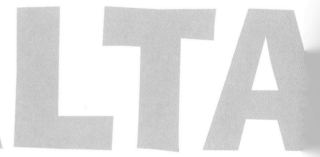

The Guevara house, which was in Alta Gracia's upper-class district and one of many almost identical residences which had been built for executives of a British railway company in the late 19th century, backed onto land which later became the local golf club. The young Che also became fairly good at that game.

By the age of 14, as his proud father would prove to visitors (and undoubtedly to Che's deep embarrassment) with before-and-after photographs from the family album, the skinny four-year-old Ernestito had grown into a muscular, handsome and very confident young man. Thanks to his father's guidance, he was also someone who could accept or reject the friendship of others with no regard for their social status, for the Guevara household was an open house to a complete cross-section of Alta Gracia society's offspring.

Despite his continued often chronic asthmatic condition, Che used his superior intelligence and quick wits to become the uncontested leader of a gang of street urchins, something his father clearly supported, as he did Che's keenness to find and take on small jobs – like helping bring in the grape harvest, a task usually the sole province of peasants. Not because they made much money (although they did supplement Che's allowance) but because they helped strengthen him physically and offered him invaluable first-hand experience of the often harsh reality of the lives lived by Argentina's peasants.

When asthma laid him low and confined him to bed for long periods, Che would dive voraciously into his father's book collection, devouring material on philosophy, mathematics, engineering, politics and sociology before spending hours discussing them with Ernesto and Celia. Although

the Guevaras were nominally Roman Catholic (Che had been baptized but never confirmed), he would come to share his father's cynical and uncompromising views on the exploitative nature of the Church:

'Christ was the greatest man on earth, but the Church ruined his preaching. The Church is the biggest business ever invented by the Jews and managed by the Italians.'

Father and son were not above joining forces to strike at those whose ideals did not match theirs. Invited to a children's birthday party at a local hotel, Che started a fight when one of the female guests remarked bitchily on his scruffy appearance. Summoned to help stop the fracas, Ernesto Sr waded into the 'rich bastards' who'd incurred Che's wrath, using a walking stick to drive his point home. Ernesto and Ernestito were both ejected by hotel staff.

With political awareness and defence of society's underdogs playing as great a part as they did in the Guevara household, it perhaps comes as no surprise to learn that Che's first display of direct-action revolt came when he was just 11 years old. During a province-wide strike by power workers which the local lighting company was trying to break by hiring blacklegs, Che marshalled his street gang into action. During one night of audacious vandalism they used catapults and stones to break all the street lights in Alta Gracia as a gesture of solidarity with the strikers.

ABOVE Ernesto (second right) and his Alta Gracia gang – ready for mischief!

ABOVE Argentina's answer to Jack Kerouac – the footloose Ernesto pictured on one of his many solo trips, 1948.

He was, by all accounts, a precociously intelligent child. Although his physical frailty meant he did not start formal schooling until he was seven (for which Celia Guevara cheerfully came into conflict with the local education authorities on a number of occasions), the basic grounding Che received from his mother at home was enough to catapult him to the top of his class every year once he began full-time education, even when his asthma forced him to miss school for long periods.

Celia taught him French, for example, a language he both loved to read and speak, often reciting long passages from memory. And the doctor father of one of his childhood friends, José Aguilar, was astonished and shocked to come across the 12-year-old Che immersed in a weighty tome by Sigmund Freud at a time when his own son was more typically and suitably immersed in comic books and the adventure novels of Jules Verne and Alexandre Dumas.

Precocious, streetwise and astute as he may have been, Che was as inconsolable as any child his age would be when the Guevaras' aged family dog died. He wasn't about to internalize his grief, however. Heading an ostentatious funeral procession of gang members through the streets of Alta Gracia, Che delivered an emotional, often tearful eulogy to his dead pet before he allowed the handmade coffin to be lowered into the grave they'd dug in a patch of scrubland!

In 1941 the Guevara family moved to the provincial capital, Córdoba, where Che was due to begin studying at a state high school. Before that happened, however, the 13-year-old casually informed his parents that he intended to spend the intervening three-months of the summer holiday exploring Argentina on his own.

Despite Celia's natural misgivings, Ernesto gave his blessing and Che set of for the first of his great adventures with only 75 pesos (about $4) as an emergency fund. A small motor had been put on his push-bike to help him up hills, and when asthma hit he simply rested by the side of the road. Sleeping in the open most of the time, with only his old leather windbreaker and cups of sweetened maté for warmth, Che worked as a humble crop-picker when his funds ran low. He was often forced to go hungry for days on end, but he completed his tour and was, as promised, back home in time for the start of the new school year.

Markedly unconventional, Che soon had two nicknames at high school: el chancho ('piggy', because of his inevitably-unkempt appearance) and el pelado, 'the shaved one', because he kept his hair cut unfashionably short after an encounter with a vagrant he'd allowed to trim his locks. The man claimed to have been a barber in better times, and Che didn't want to offend him by denying him the opportunity to display his long-lost skills.

Clearly unoffended by the 'piggy' nickname, the freelance sports reporter Che would cheerfully sign himself Chancho or Chang-Cho when he filed reports of rugby games in later years.

Che's unconventionality also extended to his openly stated opposition to the all-powerful and all-pervasive Catholic Church and his unwavering loyalty to Marxist-Socialist ideals. One of his teachers, Alfredo Pueyreddon, would later describe Che as '... **an outstanding student.**

He looked and acted much older than he was, and was clearly already grown up, with a definite personality'. However, Pueyrreddon added that Che, while mature for his age, could also be **'undisciplined and moody'.**

It was about this time that the ever-varying financial fortunes of Ernesto Sr took a dive and the family was forced to move to a smaller house. His pocket money hugely reduced, Che took a number of jobs to raise personal funds and help family resources. In spite of this double workload he finished his secondary education quickly and with honours, even though he added to his burden by joining the Comando Civico Revolucionario Monteagudo, a nationalist youth organisation which would eventually embark on a campaign of direct confrontation with the régime of dictator Juan Perón.

All the time, when his hectic school, work and growing political schedule permitted, Che would continue to hit the road. He also helped his father who, like many like-minded Argentine socialists, had begun organizing new homes and work for refugees from the post-civil war Spain of General Franco, as well as pushing himself to excel in various sports to prove that his continued susceptibility to asthma was a hurdle he could overcome.

It was Che's astonishingly objective fascination with his asthma – and his determination to find cures for the various side-effects of his drugs – which helped prompt his decision to study medicine. That, and the death of his beloved grandmother from cancer, led to his decision to enrol in the medical faculty of the University of Buenos Aires in 1947, so frustrating any hopes his father had that Che would join him in the new construction business he'd started in the capital.

Ernesto and Celia Guevara separated during this period and, while he would remain close to his father, Che elected to live with his mother. Through her he became better acquainted with a number of Argentina's leading Marxists and socialist intellectuals, though his own beliefs kept him active in the nationalist movement. This, in turn, led him to take part in a number of anti-Perón street battles and to become a prominent member of Centro Reformista, a militant university student group. Che also became a formidable, hard-tackling, even reckless member of the San Ysidro rugby team, despite having to race to the touchline from time to time when he needed to use his inhaler!

Given that Che's extra-curricular activities variously included summer jobs as a medic on a coastal freighter, a clerk in a building firm, a reporter for the nationalist newspaper, *Accion Argentina*, and as a night watchman, his progress through university was meteoric. He passed 16 major exams during one six-month period and completed six years of a scheduled seven-year course in only three. When asthma attacked most severely – which it did on 45 occasions during this time – he would simply continue studying at home, lying flat on his back to ease his breathing.

In 1950, Che tried and failed to market an insecticide he'd invented. Named in the patent he registered in Buenos Aires as Venadaval, it was his only known brush with capitalism. However, it was a project inevitably doomed by the aspiring entrepreneur's refusal to accept

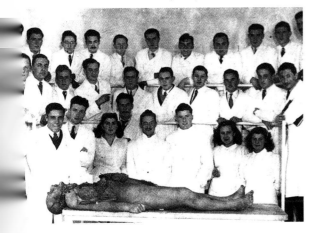

BELOW The Medical Faculty of Buenos Aires University in 1947. Ernesto is fifth from right, top row.

financial backing from his father, or his father's many business contacts.

That brief-lived venture over, Che's wanderlust once more took hold and he was easily persuaded by old friend, Alberto Granado, to join him on a remarkable odyssey. The two had first met in 1941 when Granado – later to become a distinguished biochemist and leprosy specialist – was briefly held by police for his part in a high-school revolt and Che had accompanied Alberto's brother, Tomás, on a visit to the police cells. Their friendship blossomed and became cemented when Che made a point of including San Francisco de Chañar, the remote leper hospital where Granado was working, in his various itineraries.

Granado has vivid memories of those visits and the cavalier way Che treated the matter of course revision and study for his medical degree. **'After the December examinations, instead of staying in the capital reviewing the subjects for the March exams, he would put together his knapsack, get on his motorcycle – or sometimes he just used his legs – and travel to different parts of the country.'**

Granado also had vivid evidence of Che's almost complete disregard for his own personal safety in the way he would ignore the precautions that the colony's doctors took when it came to physical contact with their patients. As he recounted to French biogragrapher Jean Cormier:

'He got a crush on a pretty young patient whose back was eaten away with leprosy . . . she asked my permission to join us at a party I was giving . . . I refused, much to Ernesto's disgust. To prove that she really was infected, I put the gorgeous Indian girl through the hot water test . . . lepers have no feeling in the infected parts of their bodies . . . she did not feel a thing, but Ernesto was furious and accused me of being a barbarian.'

So, when in October 1951 Alberto Granado suggested visiting all the countries of South America before heading for the United States, it was only natural that he should put it to Che, who had already proved himself ready to take on any dangers the back roads could present.

Granado's life was at a crossroads, having had to quit his job at the San Francisco del Chañar colony and take a lesser-paid and less challenging one at the Hospital Español in Córdoba. And Che – despite being in the midst of a love affair which he would now put on hold – was fed up with the unbroken regimen of medical school studies, hospital work and interminable examinations.

They had no time-table – save for the vague objective of Che returning to Buenos Aires by the end of 1952, in time to resume his studies for the March 1953 final university examinations – and only the sketchiest of route plans.

On January 4, 1952 the two young men climbed onto La Poderosa II, a British-manufactured Norton 500 cc motorcycle, and set off from Buenos Aires on a journey which would change the direction of Che Guevara's life forever, providing him with damning proof that the continent of South America was in desperate need of reform, and that armed revolution was the only way to achieve it.

RIGHT Ernesto, the intrepid explorer packed up and ready for yet another expedition.

On the Road

Besides fixing his future life course, the transcontinental trek with
Alberto Granado also firmly established the young Ernesto's nickname.
'Che' is a slang form of familiar address – the Argentine-Spanish
equivalent of the British 'mate' or the American 'buddy', although
it is also used as a slang hailing device in Spain and Italy.

Variously linked by entymologists to a Mapuche indian word meaning
'man', a similar Andalucian expression and a Guarani indian word for
'my', 'che' is also a generic nickname attached to Argentines in other
Spanish-speaking countries in South America. It was one Che himself
used frequently to others and, as Granado was also generally addressed
in the same fashion (although Che often referred to him, affectionately,
as Mial, a contraction of 'Mi Alberto'), he widely became known as
'Big Che' while the future revolutionary became 'Little Che'.

Before their official departure from Buenos Aires, and only after
enduring the interminable but inevitable longeurs of securing as many
travel permits, visas and other documents as they could to minimize
bureaucratic nightmares on their journey, Che headed for the coastal
resort of Mirimar and the home of Chichina, the girlfriend he was
abandoning. With him he took a winsome love-token in the small,
wriggling form of 'Come-back', a puppy he'd purchased for Chichina,
who gave him a treasured gold bracelet in return.

A dedicated diarist for much of his life, Che's surviving notes on this
first grand adventure offer an invaluable insight into the man himself,
not least because of their often ironic, self-mocking tone. Che Guevara
knew his own limitations – moral, psychological and physical – all too
well, and was ready to enumerate them with good humor and a self-
depracatory wit.

La Poderosa was not destined to carry them far. After crossing the
Andes, where it suffered a number of exasperating and time-consuming
breakdowns, the couple's motorbike finally gave up the ghost in Chile
and they were forced to continue their trip as hitch-hikers, making
meagre livings from a variety of jobs – as dishwashers, barbecue cooks,
sailors, unqualified doctors, truck drivers, security guards at a copper
mine, and even as part-time policemen and soccer team coaches.

Everywhere they went, the two young men witnessed the many
privations and injustices visited on local peasants by a combination of
grinding poverty, absentee landlords, mining and agricultural companies
and corrupt, uncaring local government officials. They also, it must be
said, found a wealth of unquestioning hospitality and friendship among
complete strangers and inevitably got into the kind of scrapes that most
young, handsome, footloose and fancy-free young men would encounter
on such a trip – whether it be with girls, because of girls, or via the
unwise and immoderate intake of local alcoholic beverages.

There were also moments of sheer farce, such as the occasion when
the duo – offered a night in a shed by a farmworker – were warned that
there was a puma at large in the area. Discovering that the bottom half

SOUTH

CUBA

GUATEMALA

atemala City

NICARAGUA

Managua

THE CARIBBEAN SEA

NORTH ATLANTIC OCEAN

PANAMA

Caracas

VENEZUELA

Bogotá

COLOMBIA

ECUADOR

Guayaquil

Iquitos   Leticia

PERU

BRAZIL

Lima   Machu Picchu

Cuzco

BOLIVIA

L. Titicaca   La Paz

AMERICA

Chuquicamata   PARAGUAY

Antofagasta

CHILE

ARGENTINA

Córdoba

PACIFIC OCEAN

URUGUAY

Valparaíso   Alta Gracia

Rosario

Santiago

Buenos Aires

Los Angeles

Valdivia

SOUTH ATLANTIC OCEAN

ABOVE A young Cuban girl circa 1950 washing clothes in water that probably constituted a health hazard.

of the shed door didn't lock, Che decided to keep his revolver by his side in case the puma came sniffing around. Near dawn he heard a scratching at the door, saw a pair of luminous eyes in the dark, let off a shot as a dark shape clambered over the door...and killed Bobby, the family dog!

Alberto and Che were also not above the odd exaggeration in their dealings with the locals they encountered. Arriving in the small Chilean port of Valdivia on a quiet Sunday, they wandered into the offices of *Correo de Valdivia*, the local newspaper, and passed themselves off as distinguished specialists en route for the leper colony on Easter Island. They gave a similar account to *El Austral* in Temuco which, when published with the headline,

'Two Argentine leprosy experts tour South America by motorbike'

ensured a new fullness in the hospitality they received.

Che, as ever, was disarmingly frank about the impact of the deception in his diary notes:

'This was our audacity in a nutshell. We, the 'experts' . . . had deigned to visit this picturesque, melancholy little town . . . soon the whole family had gathered round the article . . . and basking in their admiration, we said goodbye to these of whom we remember nothing, not even their name.'

It was this ill-deserved fame which led to an episode only a few days later when, with La Poderosa undergoing her latest batch of running repairs at a garage in the town of Lautaro, Alberto and Che were invited to a local dance by some new-found friends. Che began downing Chilean wine 'at an amazing rate', and in his drunken state got involved in a fracas with a local man's wife! The result of this incident was that Che and the woman found themselves running back to the village pursued by 'a swarm of enraged dancers!'

Maybe coincidentally (but perhaps not, given that some of the offended villagers were the same mechanics who'd been fixing her), it was during the next day that La Poderosa finally gave up the ghost and forced her riders to hitch-hike for the rest of their trip. Che was in the driver's seat when a screw worked loose on the rear brake, just as they rounded a bend and were confronted a road full of cows. Careering down-hill, they managed to avoid hitting all but the last of the herd before crashing into a bank and coming to rest between two rocks.

Miraculously unhurt, although La Poderosa was terminally bent, the couple used their newspaper clippings to persuade a German settler family to put them up. During the night, Che was stricken with diarrhoea. Not wanting, in his own words, 'to leave a souvenir in the pot under my bed', he sat on a window ledge and defacated out into the darkness. In the morning he discovered, to his horror, that a few metres under his window was a large tin roof on which peaches had been laid out for drying!

It was time for another hasty retreat.

Firemen, Stowaways & Miners

With La Poderosa an irreparable casualty (although they would try to get her fixed one more time before accepting defeat), Che and Alberto were given a lift in a truck bound for the town of Los Angeles where they would be given shelter by a Chilean army lieutenant who had fond memories of Argentine hospitality.

Those lodgings lasted only one night, however, because the very next day the two travellers moved into the local fire station, lured by the caretaker's three daughters. According to Che, they were **'prime examples of the charm of Chilean women who, ugly or pretty, have a certain spontaneity . . . which is immediately captivating.'**

He did not elaborate further, drawing a discreet veil over that part of their stay in Los Angeles. But the dynamic duo were corralled into service as volunteer firemen, despite sleeping blissfully through the clanging bells, sirens and chaos of the first emergency call which was raised during their three-day sojourn.

Typically, the two adventurers were reasonably drunk when pressed into action, but seem to have acquitted themselves well – Alberto braving what Che described as 'a twenty centimetre wall of flame' to rescue a trapped cat and accepting 'the effusive congratulations for his peerless courage' from beneath a huge borrowed helmet.

The next day, with La Poderosa on board, Che and Alberto left for Santiago, the Chilean capital, on a furniture removal truck. Their fare was to be paid in the form of their services as porters once they reached Santiago, although they managed to trick their way out of most of the work and spent much of the time gorging themselves on two kilos of grapes apiece. After finding the Argentine consulate and being lectured on their duties as roving ambassadors of their beloved country, they began the exhausting process of obtaining entry visas for Peru, documents they had not managed to pre-arrange in Buenos Aires.

On their last evening in Santiago – and typical of the happy coincidences which seemed to pepper Che Guevara's life – the impoverished couple bumped into old friends from Córdoba, the Suquiá water-polo team, who invited them to a party where the food and wine were plentiful and, more importantly, free.

Fed, watered and bidding a tearful farewell to La Poderosa for the last time, Che and Alberto hitched a lift on a truck bound for the port of Valparaíso. They had taken it into their heads to find a ship bound for Easter Island, although Che was honest enough to admit that their fascination lay less with any work or research they may do at the leper colony there than with the remote outpost's other legendary attraction: its womenfolk.

LEFT Calle Esmeralda, the main shopping street in Valparaíso, Chile.

RIGHT The massive and mysterious figures of Easter Island.

'Our imaginations soar,' he wrote, 'then stop and circle around' 'Over there, having a white boyfriend is an honour'. . . 'You don't have to work, the women do everything – you just eat, sleep and keep them happy.'

In the event, Easter Island was destined to remain a remote, untouchable paradise. Only one ship a year left Valparaíso for the colony, and they had just missed it. There were aircraft which left every month, but financial reality soon set in and they settled into a period of freeloading from a café owner who seemed happy to feed them fish dishes and soup in return for no more than the pleasure of their exotic tedium-breaking company.

While Alberto hunted for local doctors who may be able to give them some sort of work, Che set about some doctoring of his own, treating an old woman who was – like them – an almost permanent fixture at the La Gioconda café. Asthmatic, with a heart condition, she lived in complete squalor while fighting to retain what was left of the little dignity she'd enjoyed as a waitress.

Che's outrage at the old woman's situation leaped from his pen to the pages of his diary: 'In these circumstances people . . . who can't pay their way are surrounded by an atmosphere of barely-disguised acrimony. They stop being father, mother, sister or brother and become a purely negative factor in the struggle for life and, by extension, a source of bitterness for the healthy members of the community who resent their illness as if it were a personal insult to those who have to support them.'

'It is then, at the end, that we see the profound tragedy which circumscribes the life of the proletariat the world over. In these dying eyes there is a humble appeal for forgiveness and also, often, a desperate plea for solace which is lost in the void . . .'

There was anger, too, in the systems which allowed such casualties to occur, when Che concluded his account:

'How long this present order, based on an absurd idea of caste, will last I can't say, but it's time governments spent less time publicizing their own virtues and more money – much more money – funding socially useful projects.'

Che's fury was heightened by the fact that there was, in any case, very little he could offer the old woman in the way of concrete help. What he did do was advise her on diet and prescribe 'a diuretic and some asthma pills'. Working on the assumption that she and her family could probably not afford the prescription, Che slipped her a few of the precious dramamine tablets he still had to treat his own asthma, and left to re-join Alberto at La Gioconda.

The news was only so-so. Alberto had finally spoken to some of the local doctors, but they didn't have anything to offer in the way of help, save an introduction to the mayor of Valparaíso, Molinas Luco, to whom the two vagabonds had already written asking if there was any chance he could help them get to Easter Island. The mayor had not yet replied, but agreed to see them once he'd been contacted by the doctors.

The mayor was apologetic. Even though he was President of the Friends of Easter Island Society, he couldn't muster a ship out of thin air. Maybe they should come back next year when, if he was re-elected in forthcoming elections, he would be pleased to smooth their passage.

With Easter Island crossed off their ad hoc list, Che and Alberto decided to keep on heading north, towards the Chilean border with Peru. That border is straddled by a formidable barrier, however, in the shape of the Atacama Desert – a vast, rugged and inhospitable expanse it would have been foolhardy for them to attempt to cross astride La Poderosa, let alone as the raggle-taggle hitch-hikers they'd become now that their brave but battered charger had breathed her wheezy last.

The solution, when it came, seemed both obvious and obviously simple: as they didn't have enough spare funds to pay any kind of fare, they would simply work their passage to – or at least towards – Peru on one of the many merchant vessels which plied their cargo-carrying trade between Valparaíso and Chile's more northerly ports. Hitting every shipping company in town, they received nothing but directions back to the front door until a sympathetic skipper said he'd take them as far as Antofagasta, some 500 km short of the Peruvian border. There was a snag, however – he insisted that they came armed with written permission from the relevant authorities. And they, of course, refused to give the die-hards any such documentation.

It was Alberto who came up with the audacious Plan B: they would simply sneak aboard the friendly captain's boat, the San Antonio, hide in the hold until she was well out to sea, and then give themselves up. The guy wanted to help anyway, so he surely wouldn't make them walk the gangplank, or whatever it was they did to punish stowaways these days . . . would he?

It was impeccable logic and, after throwing together some bags containing only bare essentials and saying emotional farewells to the café owner and other new-found friends, Che and Alberto spent a freezing night in the shelter of a dockside crane cabin until a notoriously ill-tempered and unbribable harbour master went off duty and they could slink on board the San Antonio unchallenged.

Instead of making for the hold, the couple hid in a toilet in the officers' quarters. Bad mistake. The toilet, which had obviously been blocked for some time, stank horribly. As the sun rose, so did the smell . . . and the contents of Alberto's stomach. Finally emerging from this hell-hole to give themselves up to an astonished, but amused and understanding, skipper, they were given a meal before being allocated work-tasks. Alberto was consigned to the galley and a turgid spell as a potato peeler and dish-washer, while Che was ordered to unblock and clean the toilet, the vile contents of which had so recently been topped up by his compadre.

The journey to Antofagasta gave the intrepid stowaways time to fantasize and dream of a life devoted to wandering free, following what Che described as:

'...our true vocation [which] was to roam the highways and waterways of the world for ever. Ever curious, investigating everything we set eyes on, sniffing into nooks and crannies; but always detached, not putting down roots anywhere, not staying long enough to discover what lay beneath things: the surface was enough.'

Of course, the surface was never going to be enough and Che was quick to dismiss such thoughts as 'sentimental nonsense'. He had embarked on a journey during which he was determined to see as much as possible, and learn as much as he possibly could. He may not have been searching for proof that the political rage which burned in him was justified (he'd already experienced and seen enough on his early travels to prove that there was much that needed challenging and changing), but he was determined to see things which would confirm his right to be outraged and his need to be one of those who would challenge and change the systems which oppressed so many of the poor, the ignorant and the disadvantaged of the world.

He and Alberto were soon to witness first-hand one of the most extraordinary manifestations of one such oppressive system when, after a day-long wait in Antofagasta securing the appropriate permits, they set out to visit Chuquicamata, the legendary open-cast copper mine set in the barren heart of the Atacama Desert and from whose vast galleries a high percentage of Chile's copper is extracted. As 20 per cent of the world's entire copper stocks originate in Chile, Chuquicamata could be said to be that country's economic heart.

Hitching rides on a van and a truck, Che and Alberto spent a night in the desert with a Chilean married couple, the man a member of Chile's outlawed Communist Party who had lost many friends to government snatch squads, had himself spent three months in prison, and was even now on his way to find work in one of the notorious sulphur mines which lay in the Andes to the east where, as Che noted in his diary:

'. . . the weather is so bad and conditions so hard that you don't need a work permit and nobody asks what your politics are. The only thing that counts is the enthusiasm with which the worker ruins his health for a few meagre crumbs.'

Conditions at Chuquicamata were not much better. The safety of its ill-paid employees was the least of the Chile Exploration Company's concerns. Only supervisors wore hard-hats and ample footwear – the miners worked in dirt-encrusted jeans and singlets, with bandanas their only protection from whatever came hurtling down from higher up the vast workface. There were no safety nets or guard-rails, and only the most basic of medical facilities in an environment which resembled nothing so much as one of Hieronymus Bosch's more fevered depictions of Hell.

Che was keenly aware of the economic-political struggle which was even then being fought over Chile's copper mines, which saw a coalition of nationalist and left-wing groups which advocated nationalization pitched against one which preferred to let private, often foreign-owned, mining companies extract and market the country's single most valuable natural asset in the name of free enterprise.

The visit to Chuquicamata was brief, thanks in main to the attitude of the 'blond, efficient, arrogant managers' who told Che and Alberto that this wasn't a tourist attraction. A guide (whom Che described as 'the Yankee bosses' faithful lapdog') told them that a strike was imminent as the mine owners had just refused the workers a raise of a few centavos on what were already near-starvation wages.

Che and Alberto left Chuquicamata chastened by what they saw, with the diarist thoughtfully noting: 'Whatever the outcome of the battle, it would be well not to forget the lesson taught by the mines' graveyards, which contain but a fraction of the enormous number of people devoured by cave-ins, silicosis and the mountain's infernal climate. **'Maybe one day, some miner will joyfully take up his pick and go and poison his lungs with a smile. They say that's what it's like over there, where the red blaze dazzling the world comes from. So they say. I don't know.'**

ABOVE The Cuquicamata Processing and smelter plant, where Che and Alberto were horrified by the harsh realities of mining and the plight of the workers.

Che's scepticism about the Utopian workers-paradise image presented by the Eastern Bloc's propaganda machines was something he would never lose and, while he would espouse and fervently promote the cause of international socialism until his dying day, he never actually joined the Communist Party itself, remaining suspicious that the hierarchical structures and self-serving nepotism it often adopted once it achieved the status of national government, could be every bit as flawed as those which existed in the capitalist West.

Putting the madness of Chuquicamata behind them, Che and Alberto set their faces north, towards the border with Peru. It was time to push on once more and find new adventures.

Incas, Conquistadors & Rip-off Routines

Baked by searing heat in the day and reduced to shivering, frozen
bundles at night, Che and Alberto made it across the mountainous
Atacama Desert into Peru by walking at night and picking up rides
whenever they could from the few battered, ancient and invariably
overloaded trucks which hauled their rickety way up and down the often
precipitous roads some intrepid souls had managed to blast out of this
unremitingly harsh terrain. More than once they had to help push ailing
vehicles up to the next summit.

Occasionally riding with indian workers, the two Argentines
invariably had their attempts at conversation – and their overtures of
friendship – rebuffed with stone-faced silence. Che soon came to realise
it was nothing personal. The indians were so accustomed to being treated
like dirt by everyone higher up the social scale (which was pretty well
everyone else in Chile and Peru), their reserve was an entrenched
defense mechanism founded on long and bitter experience.

The same was not true of the people in the small towns and villages
where they stopped, although the shortage of maté was a hardship both
men found increasingly tiresome. But the warmth of their welcome –
which was all the more fulsome once Alberto waved his doctor's
certificate about – more than compensated for that, especially when

ABOVE The Plaza in Cuzco, seen from the tower of the cathederal, 1954.

they were invited to share the poor fare on which these people subsisted. Che and Alberto paid what they could when they could but, more often than not, their attempts to offer money would be graciously refused. Time and again Che could not help but be struck by the selfless generosity of those who obviously had so little.

He was also amused by the images of Argentina – and the boundless generosity apparently lavished on its citizens by the benevolent double act of President Juan Perón and his wife, the beautiful and saintly Evita – which these peasants had somehow accumulated.

Not wishing to offend their listeners with alternative versions of the régime they both despised and which they had physically fought in the streets of Buenos Aires, Che and Alberto regaled their hosts with what they obviously wanted to hear – Technicolor and CinemaScope tales of this mythical land of boundless milk and honey – and even promised to send one aged Perón fan a copy of the Argentine Constitution, which included a declaration of rights for old people.

Stopping by the shores of the sacred Lake Titicaca on the Peruvian border with Bolivia, for a brief spot of tourism, they were 'adopted' by a succession of civil guards who took a fancy to these odd-looking Argentine doctors and helped speed their way towards Cuzco, the heart and ancient capital of the Incan civilisation which held sway in those parts for some 1,500 years, stretching – at its peak – from southern Venezuela in the north to mid-Chile in the south and incorporating parts of modern-day Ecuador, Bolivia, Brazil and Argentina to the east.

By 1532, when an invasion force of only 200 Spanish conquistadores launched an invasion to overthrow and subdue the Incas with consummate ease, that empire boasted some 12,000,000 subjects, incoporating 100 ethnic groups who spoke 20 different languages. Ironically, it was the Incas' feat of developing a series of interlinked roadways which facilitated the invaders' progress and the rapidity of their conquest, which was absolute.

Stripping the empire of its most valuable gold and silver artefacts, and forcibly imposing Christianity on a people whose traditional religion included the worship of Inti, the sun god, and fetishistic sacrificial tribute to other gods of nature such as Viracocha (a creator god) and the rain god Apu Illapu, the conquistadores subdued the population into a state of near-slavery and a return to a rootless, near-nomadic existence as whole swathes of tribal lands were confiscated for Spanish estates.

Two weeks in the faded splendor of Cuzco and a trek to the long-abandoned ruins of the fabled Incan citadel atop the mountain of Machu Picchu, provided ample fuel for Che's imagination.

Paradoxically, while he railed against the Spanish destruction of the Incas' most noble temples and palaces and the use of their huge stones in the construction of new cathedrals and churches for the worship of their imported religion, Che could also thrill to 'the formidable courage of the soldiers' who conquered the region. Strolling through the most-obviously

Spanish section of Cuzco with its monuments, museums and libraries, he admitted it would be easy to submit to the urge

'to don armour and, astride a sturdy powerful steed, cleave a path through the defenceless flock of naked indians whose human wall crumbles under the four hooves of the galloping beast.'

It is difficult to explain such a dramatic contradiction in his responses, but entirely possible that Che himself recognized the paradox for what it was – a conflict between the educated, politically sensitive half of him which recognized and abhorred the legacy of an imperialist invasion which had created a despised sub-class out of indians whose cultural heritage had been systematically destroyed, and the inherently-proud Spanish side of him which could respect the achievements of those conquisatore pioneers, so overwhelmingly victorious despite apparently insuperable odds.

There is no doubt, however, that the awe-inspiring sight of the Incan ruins which dominate the rugged countryside around the one-time capital fascinated and enthralled Che. Typically, he quickly amassed and absorbed a wealth of knowledge of Incan history, myths and legends, the art and architecture – information which he would, in later times and different places, draw on to become a sometime lecturer to supplement his always-stretched financial resources!

His two principal sources of information and inspiration were a Dr Hermosa – to whom Alberto presented a letter of introduction he'd been given by a mutual family friend in Buenos Aires – and a Señor Soto, manager of an hotel near Machu Picchu. An admirer of one of the eminent leprologists with whom Alberto had studied, Hermosa was a mine of information on Peruvian society, both ancient and modern.

For his part, Señor Soto invited Che and Alberto to be his personal unpaying guests for a few days after they joined in a game of soccer with some locals, and was impressed when Che let slip that he had played semi-professional first division football in Argentina. His expertise lay in Incan history, and the two Argentines were enthralled with the stream of knowledge he willingly imparted to an audience who obviously cared enough to listen intently, unlike the Yankee tourists who flew to Lima, came to photograph Machu Picchu and returned home without taking time to look at the real people of Peru.

Bidding regretful farewells to Cuzco, Che and Alberto hit out northwards after a south-west detour to Abancay, the best pick-up spot for long-distance trucks. Their objective was the town of Huancarama, near which stood the noted leper colony of Huambo. Alberto was determined to spend some time there and, as ever, came armed with letters of introduction from Argentine specialists to the resident doctor, Señor Montejo.

During the trek to Huancarama, Che was hit by the first of what would be a number of severe asthma attacks. Without the ampules of adrenalin which would have relieved his condition, he was barely able to stand when they finally arrived, and spent a sleepless night wrapped in a

LEFT The legendary Incan citadel of Machu Picchu fired Ernesto's imagination and anger.

borrowed police blanket, watching a rainstorm and chain-smoking cigarettes of dark, almost black tobacco which helped relieve his fatigue. As dawn broke, Alberto located some adrenalin and that, plus a few aspirins, brought Che round.

He was appalled at what he and Alberto found when they finally reached the leper colony. Although the staff worked tirelessly for little pay and no recognition, the Huambo compound consisted of a central adobe building, most of which was taken up by a ward holding 31 patients. The sanitary conditions were terrible, and while Che thought that the indian patients (whose hygiene and personal sanitation habits were pretty unsophisticated) might have been able to accept such surroundings, he was sure that better-educated mestizos (mixed race) inmates must have found it 'very unpleasant'.

As far as he could see, the clinic's drug treatment program was its only saving grace. Señor Montejo was doing what he could, but had the extra inevitable burden of local ignorance and fear to contend with as he attempted to make his poor little colony work. When he'd first arrived to establish the place some years earlier, none of the hotels in Huancarama would give him a room. Only recently – when a patient needed an operation 'too serious to do on the kitchen table without surgical equipment', his requests to use the facilities of a nearby hospital ('in the morgue, if need be') were rejected. The patient died.

Although a new and bigger facility was being built a few kilometres away from Huambo, Che noted that although it would have improved santitation for the 250 or so patients it could hold, it did not have any laboratory or surgical facilities and, to make matters worse, was sited in an area plagued by mosquitoes.

After two days at Huambo, Che's asthma worsened and the two travellers began another long and exhausting trek to the town of Andahuaylas, where he was hospitalized. Treated, rested, pretty well recovered and equipped with replacement drugs, he and Alberto continued north, increasing poverty firing their creative juices to develop a hard-luck routine guaranteed to persuade some gullible stranger into buying them a drink, and then some food. Che called it 'our brilliant anniversary routine.'

One of the vagrants would say something in a loud voice, exaggerating the Argentine accent and conspicuously using the word *che*. The 'mark' would ask where they were from and a conversation would begin, during which Alberto would suddenly ask what the date was. When told it, he would sigh and say that it was exactly a year to the day since they'd started their trip, sigh again and say (in an audible aside to Che) that it was a shame they couldn't afford to celebrate such an auspicious event.

The victim's generous, sympathetic offer of a drink would be finally, reluctantly, accepted, but Che would refuse a second on the grounds that, in Argentine, it was the custom not to drink without food. 'Just how much we eat depends on what we think we can get away with', he noted. But the technique, apparently, never failed.

Sheer bluff, bravado and bare-faced cheek was the other approach. They would locate the local hospital, find a doctor and Che would

brazenly announce: 'I'm a medical student, my friend is a biochemist. We are both Argentine and we're hungry. We want to eat.' Stunned by this basic full-frontal attack, the doctor would invariably guide them to the canteen and feed them!

It was simple, but it was effective. And it helped them get to their next objective – Lima, the capital of Peru, where they wanted to meet Dr Hugo Pesce, the original founder of the Huambo leper colony and someone Alberto was especially keen to spend time with on this leg of their journey, both as an important source of scientific information and as someone who could maybe help smooth their way onwards.

Lepers, Mambo-Tango and Miami

Hugo Pesce would turn out to be a combination of saviour and inspiration for Che and Alberto – a saviour because his hospitality was generous to the point of lavish, and inspiration because he furnished Alberto with priceless introductions to other eminent South American leprologists and hospitals, leading to him settling in Venezuela, where he would become a noted and gifted specialist in his chosen field.

Holder of the Chair of Tropical Medicine in Lima University, Pesce had been forced to transfer to Huambo, 800 kilometres from the capital, when his progressive (left-wing) political views met the disfavour of Peru's authoritarian president, General Manuel Odría, who'd seized power in 1948. With nothing but the most basic medical equipment at his disposal, Pesce triumphantly wrote a seminal monograph on the physiology of the local inhabitants, made the first diagnosis of exanthematic typhoid, classified three types of phlebotomy (the surgical opening of a vein as medical treatment) and designed the surgical lancet which now bore his name.

Confronted by the endemic leprosy of the region, he founded the Huambo leper colony, and the international acclaim which greeted the various papers Pesce published in medical journals led to him being given back his university post. A fund of enthralling autobiographical adventure stories, Pesce made the mistake of proudly presenting the Argentines with a copy of his memoirs, *Latitudes of Silence* – a tome which recounted those same escapades, but in a turgid, almost unreadable prose.

Only too aware of Che's tendency to express his views with blunt candour, regardless of the consequences, Alberto made him promise not to refer to the subject. On their last night in Lima, however, they were dining chez Pesce when their host began to press for their impressions of his magnum opus. Keeping his word, Che delved into his plate of stew while 'Mial' blustered on with a series of anodyne compliments which skillfully evaded the harsh truth.

Pesce was pleased, but was determined to have Che's opinion too. He pressed and pressed until he got it, then shrank further and further into his chair as his young guest itemized the book's defects remorselessly, concluding with a withering: **'I find it incredible that you, a man of the left, should have written such a decadent book, which suggests no way out for the indian and the half-caste!'**

As Che and Alberto walked back to their lodgings at the Hospital de Guía, a leprosy clinic, the older man finally broke the embarrassed silence to remonstrate with his companion. Che was apologetic. **'But you saw how I tried to say nothing in the beginning,'** he told Alberto. **'I made every effort not to answer . . .'**

Alberto had just had further evidence that, while Che would undoubtedly be hurt at having to offend someone he admired, having to tell a lie would have upset him even more. It was a Guevara characteristic which would make him as many enemies as friends along the way as his

LEFT Iquitos, Peru, the floating suburb of Belen on the Amazon with canoes in the foreground and huts in the background.

ABOVE The main square in Iquitos, Peru – where Ernesto was confined to a hospital bed for a couple of days.

bluntness – refreshing in a usually mealy-mouthed political arena – could also be construed as offensive hectoring, and evidence of a bully-boy trait many found both unpleasant and needless.

Nothing if not a walking set of contradictions, Che could just as readily display some of the more engaging aspects of his personality – his deep compassion for others, his determination to tear down the barriers which most of society placed between them and the less fortunate, and his readiness to act while others stood by considering their options.

These would all be evidenced in the San Pablo leper colony, which was located near Iquitos, at the confluence of the Pastaza, Napo and Ucayali rivers in north-east Peru. Che and Alberto had reached Iquitos after a long, mosquito-bedevilled road and river expedition during which Che's asthma had re-surfaced with a vengeance, his supply of adrenalin ran dangerously low, and he survived on a diet of rice and maté – all he could keep down in his permanently nauseous and dangerously weakened state.

Their funds boosted by 100 Peruvian *soles* and a primus stove – the results of an impromptu collection held by Hospital de Guía patients in gratitude for the time they'd spent keeping them company, listening to soccer games on the radio, or simply talking to them like ordinary human beings – the adventurers had been able to afford third-class tickets on a ferry steamship which worked the Ucayali River as far as Iquitos. Those funds had been further improved when Alberto enjoyed a winning streak at cards. From Iquitos they would have to find a smaller boat to take them downriver to San Pablo.

Armed with fulsome letters of introduction from Dr Pesce (happily secured before Che was persuaded to deliver his literary review of *Latitudes of Silence*), they boarded the little *El Cisne* ('The Swan') for a last night and day of unrelenting mosquito attack before they finally reached the leper colony of which a Dr Bresciani was the medical director. Before that, however, Che was confined to a hospital bed in Iquitos for a couple of days while his condition was stabilized.

San Pablo was a refuge for 'incurable' lepers, the worst of them severely mutilated with fingers, toes, entire limbs and parts of their faces eaten away. Whole families lived in the heart of the colony, for parents refused to abandon their children, and these formed a tight-knit community which made and sold 'traditional native' artefacts, fishing hooks, nets, and ran small businesses successful enough for their owners to afford motor boats.

Set on the swampy banks of the Amazon – and therefore prone to flooding – San Pablo housed about a thousand patients, and appeared to the newcomers like any riverside jungle community with its huts on stilts, and canoes and other small boats bustling to and fro from a landing stage loaded with produce that included root vegetables, fruit, and fresh and dried fish.

Outside the main colony, and the site of what Che and Alberto named 'the striptease joint' (a cleansing facility in which one donned protective clothing – including gloves and surgical masks – before entering the lepers' areas, and changed back on the way out, after a thorough shower

and scrubbing), lived the colony's staff, a two hundred-strong army of doctors, dentists, nuns, monks and priests.

Deep in the heart of the colony was a separate 'no-go zone' where the most seriously affected – and therefore deemed the most contagious – lepers were housed. Needless to say, it was this area of San Pablo into which Alberto and his 'assistant' headed at once, despite the protestations and dire warnings of Dr Bresciani's helpers.

It did not take Alberto long to establish that the form of leprosy these unfortunates had contracted was not contagious. Casting off their own protective clothing, the young Argentines also removed many patients' bandages and touched their mangled bodies.

Their arrival, their apparent fearlessness and their obvious sympathy for the people of San Pablo, would make an enormous impact on the colony, not least because it would help transform the long-term treatment given to men and women who had previously been treated like medieval 'untouchables', the lost and the damned of biblical legend.

Moreover, Che and Alberto revolutionized attitudes by the simple device of organizing soccer games between patients and staff. They always turned out on the patients' teams, so forging a deeper emotional link with the lepers. But the greatest breakthrough came when Che (under Alberto's watchful surveillance) operated to remove a nodule which was preventing a patient from bending his arm – a problem which could, untreated, have led to quite serious long-term disability, and even the loss of that arm. The man's recovery raised Che's stock with the indians immeasurably, as did his habit of taking his meals with them, another revolutionary gesture.

Many years later, Silvio Lozano, the leper on whom Che had operated, was tracked down by journalist Andy Dressler.

'He saved me,' Lozano told Dressler. 'It was the beginning of a new age at the leper colony, the surgical instruments never got a chance to rust! Later, when he was Minister of the Economy in Cuba, he wrote me a letter asking me how I was.'

Not only had Che saved Lozano, enabling him to eventually own and run his own bar, but he had found time to send him a message many years later when one would imagine there were much more pressing demands on his time. Lozano's bar, by the way, was called Che.

After a couple of weeks at San Pablo, Che and Alberto had to move on. Hearing that their plan was to follow the Amazon east, the lepers built them an elaborate raft which was promptly named *Mambo-Tango* – Mambo for the current dance craze, Tango after the national dance of the young doctors' country. The naming ceremony took place on June 14, Che's birthday, during the course of a riotous party which featured vast quantities of pisco, a Peruvian gin-like drink which rendered both Che and Alberto senseless.

There was to be another party five days later, when Che and Alberto set sail on *Mambo-Tango*, the craft's hut-like shelter laden with all the provisions they could have needed: pineapples, dried fish and meat, sausages, butter, two live chickens plus, along with a lantern, petrol for their primus stove and an all-important mosquito net.

Their send-off was memorable, as Che would recount in a letter to his mother, written on board *Mambo-Tango* while Alberto rowed and steered:

'As a farewell, the lepers formed a band. The accordionist was missing the fingers of his right hand and had replaced them with sticks tied to his wrists. The singer was blind, and almost all of them were disfigured. All of this by the light of lanterns and flares . . . like something out of a horror movie, but it will nevertheless remain one of the most beautiful memories of my life.'

Three days later the adventurers arrived in Leticia, an Amazon River port which stands at the junction of the borders of Peru, Colombia and Brazil, but only after they had managed to ground *Mambo-Tango* on a sandbank. Discovering to their frustration that they had missed Leticia in the dark, and were now infact in Brazil – without the necessary documentation of course – they were forced to struggle back against the current in a borrowed canoe.

Haggling 50 per cent off the listed air fare to the Colombian capital, Bogotá, the duo learned that they would have to wait almost two weeks before the next flight arrived. Down to their last handfuls of small coins of various denominations after stumping up their fares in the same fashion, the stop-over in Leticia looked like being a grim, fun-free zone until a police colonel, who'd heard exaggerated reports of their soccer careers in Argentina, offered them a job coaching the local team.

According to Che, although the idea was to lick them into enough shape so they didn't make fools of themselves in an upcoming tournament, the team was so bad that he and Alberto decided to play too, **'with the brilliant result that what was considered the weakest team went into the one-day chamionship totally reorganized, got to the final and only lost on penalties. Alberto was inspired . . . with his spot-on passes . . . and I saved a penalty which will go down in the history of Leticia.'**

Feeling like they had 'already been around the world twice', Che and Alberto finally reached Bogotá, discovered that they couldn't even beg a room or bed in the university, but were eventually housed by a local leprosy service which, once they'd had the full benefit of the now-perfected Big Che-Little Che charm offensive, offered them jobs!

While Alberto was only too keen to accept for professional reasons, Che wanted to push on to Venezuela, their next intended port of call. He didn't like Colombia much, and Bogotá not at all, describing the atmosphere as suffocating.

Eight days after that letter was penned, Che and Alberto crossed the border between Colombia and Venezuela on foot, their decision to quit Bogotá hastened by an encounter with Colombian police who expressed their disquiet at a rough and wholly innocent sketch which Che had just traced in roadside dust by muscling in, rifle butts raised.

Reaching Caracas after an arduous, exhausting and cramped trip in an overcrowded and decrepit mini-bus (during which Che had a serious asthma attack that Alberto relieved with adrenalin injections), the brave pioneers went their separate ways – Alberto to the leprology job which would establish his reputation, and Che to one last bizarre adventure before he finally made it back to Buenos Aires for his final exams. It was one which was to offer him his first eye-opening glimpse of el Norte, in the surreal surroundings of Miami, playground of the rich.

An old business contact of his father had a racehorse stud and transportation business in Caracas and invited Che to help take a number of animals by plane to Florida. After a one-day stopover in Miami, the plane was due to return to Caracas before flying on to Buenos Aires. Che accepted with alacrity – not only would he achieve his ambition of taking a look at the Evil Empire (albeit a very brief one), but he'd get paid and have a lightning lift back home into the bargain.

As ever, it didn't work out quite like that. The transporter plane developed engine problems en route for Miami and was grounded for a month, stranding a nearly-penniless Che in a city notorious for its high cost of living and its lack of sympathy for those unable to afford it. Lacking even the price of bus fares, Che would walk daily from his small

ABOVE Limbo dancing on the beaches of Florida – where a penniless Che spent one month enjoying himself.

hotel into the centre of Miami and from there to the beaches – a distance of some 15 kilometres.

According to his father, Che was rarely able to hitch a ride but, far from being outraged by the opulence and holiday-making indolence which surrounded him, enjoyed himself as much as he could. It is strange to consider that, even as Che made the best of his situation by working on his tan (the sunshine, at least, was free), he was only 120 kilometres or so away from the shores of Cuba, the island which was destined to play such an all-important role in his future.

At the beginning of September, 1952, the Guevara family were assembled en masse at Ezeiza airport to welcome their prodigal son home. Typically, the transporter plane was two anxious hours late arriving at Buenos Aires. But, after eight long months on the road, Ernesto Guevara once more set foot on Argentine soil, his eyes opened by the sights he'd seen on his travels with Alberto Granado, his mind firmly set on an overwhelming desire to add whatever weight he could to the wheels of much-needed change.

Roaming, Revolution & Romance

Returning to his studies with all the ferocious diligence of old, in March 1953 – less than six months after returning home – Che passed a record 12 examinations to become Ernesto Guevara, MD. It was a remarkable achievement, all things considered, for while his work as Alberto's 'assistant' obviously provided him with valuable hands-on experience, he had lost a phenomenal amount of time on many other important aspects of his degree courses, not least lectures, seminars and personal tuition sessions. If anyone doubted his ability to make up what was, in effect, a lost year, Che proved them wrong in triumphant style.

Any hopes his parents may have had that Che would finally settle down to a brilliant medical career specializing in allergies were shattered only four months later when he took off again, initially by train to Bolivia with a medical student, Carlos 'Calica' Ferrer, but with the eventual aim of rejoining Alberto Granado in the Venezuelan leper colony which now employed him.

However, while in the Bolivian administrative capital, La Paz, Che met and befriended another restless, footloose compatriot, a young lawyer named Ricardo Rojo. The two chanced to meet at a swish cocktail party at which, Rojo later recalled, Che had arrived wearing **'a filthy brown jacket, rumpled shirt, and dirt-spotted shoes which had no trace of leather left'.** Although clean-shaven, Che had grown his hair long and had become even more voluble on the subject of the injustices he'd witnessed on his travels, not least the appalling conditions in which Bolivia's miners lived and worked for US-owned mineral companies. Nevertheless, Rojo claimed, Che appeared to have no loyalties to any one party.

Attempting to gain a better picture of Bolivia's unsettled political situation (a popular uprising had recently installed the supposedly liberal government of Paz Estenssoro), Che and Calica secured an audience with the minister responsible for indian affairs. At the Ministry entrance was an endless silent line of native Bolivians, hoping to register claims to the land they'd been promised in new agrarian reforms. Before they were allowed to enter the hallowed portals, however, a Ministry employee sprayed every one of them from a can of DDT insecticide.

Enraged by this, Che heard the minister's grand pronouncements of change and improvement with a fair degree of scepticism, convinced that if the original peoples of Bolivia could not be released from this ingrained arrogance – if this 'revolution' could not give them back their basic dignity – it was a revolution doomed to failure.

Che, Rojo and four other Argentines decided to hitch-hike to Peru, but only got as far as Guayaquil, Ecuador, where they managed to obtain six berths on a cargo ship (ironically, it was owned by the hated and ubiquitous United Fruit Company) bound for Panama. At the last minute, however, Che decided not to go with them, saying he'd get to Panama on his own. He never did show up there, and it would be some months before Rojo – who was hitching a car ride from Guatemala with

ABOVE Bolivian workers hand-sorting tungsten in the mines at Chojilla circa 1950.

two brothers who were returning to Argentina from a stint as teachers in the United States – would chance across Che, who had walked hundreds of miles from Panama with a student companion and was attempting to hitch-hike on the Pan-American Highway!

Dressed in filthy rags and in the midst of a serious asthma attack, Che and his companion gratefully accepted the offer of a ride to Managua where, after Ricardo and Walter Beveraggi Allende – one of the teaching brothers – had sold the car and given them a change of clothes, Che, Eduardo Garciá (the student from La Plata who'd been Che's hitch-hiking companion) and Walter's brother, Domingo, decided to push on for Guatemala, once more on foot.

Allende would encounter Che again from time to time as he drifted on his own way across South America and remains struck by the belief that Che seemed to feel personally responsible for all the injustices he'd witnessed,

'full of fight and devotion to some inner ideal.'

On one occasion, while they were crossing a United Fruit plantation, Allende and Che came across a group of children with the distended bellies of the severely undernourished.**'Che went into one of his rages'**, Allende recalled. **'He cursed everybody from God to North American exploiters, and wound up with a frightening asthma attack lasting two hours.'**

When Rojo brought Che up to date on conditions in Guatemala, where the new régime of Jacobo Arbenz had seized and nationalized land owned by United Fruit and other US multinationals with terrible track records of employee exploitation, his friend was suitably outraged. As was his way, Che immediately determined to go to Guatemala and offer his services to the Arbenz government. In December 1953, he arrived at the home of Juan Angel Muñoz Aguilar, a Honduran who was a good friend of Guatemala's ex-President, Juan José Arevalo, and married to an Argentine girl whose family Che knew well.

Finding work selling religious artefacts (which was ironic, given his deep and abiding hatred of the Catholic Church and his perception of it as a principal player in the game to keep the masses ignorant, compliant, poor and huddled), Che moved into a cheap and flea-infested boarding house where conditions and a poor diet combined to worsen his asthma and make him lose a dangerous amount of weight. In true Che style, however, friends recall him reading on furiously, even when confined to bed, his atomizer always at hand.

Soon after his arrival in Guatemala City, Muñoz Aguilar introduced Che to Hilda Gadea Acosta, the young woman who would become his wife. A Peruvian by birth, Hilda was a member of that country's outlawed Aprista Party17 – the same political group which claimed the membership and loyalties of Dr Hugo Pesce, eminent leprologist, benevolent dinner host and would-be best-selling author. Nicknamed 'la China' because of the slanted eyes which betrayed her indian ancestry, she had trained as an economist, joined the Aprista Youth Movement and, via her oratory skills, became not only the youngest member of the National Executive Committee, but also sat on its board of directors.

Three years older than Che, Hilda possessed a vitality which attracted him at once, though he was alone among her circle of friends in that he did not fully share her optimism and confidence in the future. Unlike Che, for whom clothes and physical appearance were of no importance, Hilda was invariably well and elegantly dressed. Although he was clearly struck by her on their first meeting, Hilda considered Che far too good-looking to be intelligent, and somewhat too self-assured, even arrogant.

A friendship blossomed nevertheless, and when Che had finished reading her copy of Mao Tse-tung's *New China*, he promised to take her to see the Great Wall. Both of them would make that trip, but it would be many years later and it would not be together.

Through Hilda, Che was introduced to members of the July 26 Movement based in Guatemala. This group of exiled Cubans – so called to commemorate the day in 1953 when dissidents led by a young lawyer, Fidel Castro, launched an attack on Moncada Barracks – were only too happy to regale the young Che with tales of their brave leader, then still languishing in a Cuban prison.

Che had, in fact, met July 26 exiles before (in San José, Costa Rica), but while he had heard their stories and sympathised with their aims to oust the oppressive régime of President Fulgencio Batistá, he had not formally allied himself to their cause. Unlike Hilda, who was already a committed Castroist, Che confined his energies to listening, learning and questioning the exiles when they met.

On one of these occasions – a picnic party – Che proposed to Hilda for the first time, countering her amused refusal with: 'You are healthy, your parents are healthy, so there's nothing to stop us marrying . . . !'

In February 1954 the clouds which had been gathering over Jacobo Arbenz's little libertarian state began to break, along with strong rumors that Guatemala was about to be invaded by forces who were known to have US support. Che was desperate to become one of the defenders who would repel these imperialist lackeys, but in the lull before the coming storm he did unpaid volunteer work in a hospital – his application for a paid post having been rejected because he was not a member of the Communist Party.

By June, when the threat of invasion solidified into an imminent reality, Hilda was trying to persuade Che to go to Mexico, especially since his Guatemalan residence permit had expired. Introduced to an East German 'Mr Fix-it' who offered him a Mexican entry visa on condition that he joined the Communist Party, an angry Che elected to stay, volunteered his services as a doctor and received some basic military training from officers of a youth brigade.

On June 26, President Arbenz resigned, throwing his country into a panic and the doors wide open for the forces of Colonel Castillo Armas to invade. Amid the chaos, Hilda was stunned when Che proposed,

ABOVE Ernesto and Hilda were married in August 1955. Here they are pictured at the Mayan temples during their Honeymoon in Mexico.

ABOVE This photo, taken in a cell they shared, is the earliest known of Fidel (left) and Che together. They were arrested by Mexican police in June 1956, after Guevara joined Castro's force in Mexico.

unsuccessfully, for a second time. Intending to escape to Argentina, where she planned to stay with Che's mother, Hilda was arrested as she returned to her apartment. When Che heard the news, he made for the Argentine embassy and claimed sanctuary. He was reluctantly given it, but would spend nearly three months paying his keep as a kitchen help.

A few weeks after her arrest, Hilda recalled that she had met Castillo Armas, the new president, some years earlier. Managing to make a telephone call from the prison governor's office, she demanded an audience with Armas, at which point the governor ordered her release. Trying to join Che at the Argentine embassy, she was turned away and began to live with as low a profile as possible to avoid re-arrest.

In early September, President Juan Perón ordered a plane to fly from Buenos Aires to Guatemala and airlift his stranded diplomats and other compatriots home. Che refused to go, taking a train to Mexico instead, this time with papers which didn't need him to swear fealty to the communists. Hilda saw him off, headed back to the friend's house in which she'd been staying, and was promptly arrested by two officials who told her she was to be deported – to Mexico!

After an adventurous journey (she was re-arrested in the border town of Malacatan, bribed her way out of prison and crossed into Mexico by swimming across a river), Hilda arrived in Mexico City to be reunited with Che, who now had a new side-kick – a young Guatemalan revolutionary, Roberto Caceres, whom he'd met on his way north.

Caceres, who would later be popularly known as el Patojo ('the waddling one') when he played an active and heroic part in the Cuban revolution, was already sharing a flat with Che. It would be he who introduced Che to Raúl Castro, brother and chief lieutenant of the legendary Fidel. Soon after, in July 1955, Che would finally meet Fidel himself, recent beneficiary of an amnesty declared by Cuba's President Fulgencio Batistá, the man whose US-backed régime the young revolutionary was determined to overthrow.

Before that, however, there was the small matter of Che finally persuading Hilda to become his wife. The plans they made included a honeymoon in China and a trip to view the Great Wall. Inevitably, that failed to materialize: the only cheap tickets they could buy clashed with their wedding date, August 8. Instead, they honeymooned – before their wedding – in the town of Cuernavaca, south-west of Mexico City, Che filling their room with flowers and love poems. Hilda was already pregnant and Che was delighted with life.

The encounter which would irrevocably change that life took place in the second week of July, at the apartment of Maria Antonia Sanchez Gonzalez, a Cuban married to a Mexican. To observers it seemed as if Fidel Castro and Che Guevara 'recognised' each other as kindred spirits – even long-lost soul brothers – from the moment they were introduced.

From 10pm, when they first shook hands, until way past dawn, they discussed revolution, their beliefs, their hopes and fears. When Che departed, he had sworn himself into the July 26 Movement, accepting the post of their only doctor. Although he didn't know it, he was about to be involved in one of the most audacious adventures of modern times.

ABOVE Already on his way as a revolutionary – the young beardless Fidel Castro during a tribunal by governmental soldiers in which he was being prosecuted for his part in an attack on the barracks – La Moncada – 1953.

Castro soon became a frequent guest at the Guevara home, where he inevitably reviewed his plans to invade Cuba over dinner. The two men's friendship deepened and solidified, not least because Che was prepared to give the dogmatic Castro as good as he got in debate – a rare experience for the ex-lawyer, who was accustomed to his forceful views being accepted without confrontation. Better still, while he and Che could spend hours battling over fine political points, it was clear that their differences were never based on objectives, only how those objectives would best be achieved.

Raúl Castro was Che's best man when he married Hilda. Fidel was asked to perform the role but it was decided that his participation should be restricted to that of party guest, for security reasons.

From the beginning of his relationship with Castro, Che had made it clear that he intended to be a combatant doctor. He wanted to be able to attack and defend, as well as cure and mend. No matter that he had no guerrilla experience – the small Cuban revolutionary force was still undergoing training at the hands of a Spanish Loyalist general, Alberto Bayo, at a secret base on Chapultepec Lake.

Donning camouflage uniform and armed with one of the guns the group had amassed, Che Guevara started learning fast.

The Great Adventure

Che had needed little persuasion to pitch in his lot with Fidel Castro. As he would recall in later memoirs, Che's experiences all over Latin America, not least during the Guatemalan coup, had combined to confirm his determination to join almost any revolution against tyranny, especially if it enabled him to hit at those he considered the real enemies – the CIA, US-owned international conglomerates, and the American imperialism which installed and supported repressive régimes around the world. While he had never even been to Cuba, he knew the island to be a prime example of US domination, and Batistá a puppet president whose strings were in urgent need of cutting.

There was also the small matter of Fidel Castro's charisma. Castro was, in Che's own words:

'an extraordinary man. He confronted and solved the most impossible problems. He had an unshakeable faith that once he left exile in Mexico and arrived in Cuba he would fight, and would win that fighting. I shared his optimism. It was imperative to do something, to struggle, to achieve. It was imperative to stop crying and fight!'

ABOVE Castro and fellow fighters at their camp in the mountains of Sierra Maestra – 9 June 1957.

That fight began on November 25, 1956 when the pathetically small guerrilla force of only 82 poorly-armed men set sail for Cuba aboard a 62-foot rustbucket of a yacht, the *Granma*. Their departure had been delayed by six weeks when Castro and many of the would-be insurgents – including Che, who lacked residence papers – were arrested by Mexican police. Substantial bribes secured their release but reduced their ability to buy more arms and ammunition.

Che was seen off by the by-now heavily pregnant Hilda, who would give birth to a daughter, Hilda Beatriz (but called 'Hildita' by her parents) while her husband was embroiled in the early struggle to gain a foothold in the wilds of Cuba. Hilda had, as she said later, 'lost my husband to the Cuban Revolution'.

That revolution almost ended before it really began. The six days Castro's pitiable force spent on storm-tossed waters (with Dr Guevara working overtime treating widespread and messy seasickness), ended with a crunching, uncontrolled landfall on December 2 at Las Colorados and an almost immediate strike by Cuban ground forces who'd been alerted by a coastguard.

With most of their guns and ammunition lost – along with the bulk of Che's medical supplies – they headed inland through mangrove swamps towards the relative safety of the Sierra Maestra mountains, were betrayed by a guide and attacked again, this time by Cuban air force planes, as they crossed a sugarcane plantation. Only twenty men survived to form the nucleus of Castro's rebel army, the others having been killed, wounded or captured by Batistá's troops.

It was during that second action, at Alegría de Pío, that Che was

ABOVE Fidel Castro – Havana 1960.

CASTRO

ABOVE The rebels under cover in the mountains – June 1957.

forced to make a fateful decision about his role in the revolution. Racked with pain from an asthma attack, he was resting by a tree when the government forces launched their offensive. One of his comrades dropped an ammunition box in the panic and ran off to safety. Che had a clear choice: pick up the vital ammunition and join the escape, or carry his rucksack of medicines. He chose the ammunition.

Despite being wounded in the neck and chest, Che managed to crawl to the cover of the canefield and drag himself towards Castro's position. It was only the first of a number of times that his bravery, and his apparent disregard of personal safety, would culminate in injury. As the only doctor in Fidel's little army, it was always a case of 'Physician, heal thyself', even when the damage was as serious as an M-l bullet in the foot. There was also the dangerous debilitation of long-untreated asthma, not to mention the fact that he had become allergic to mosquito bites which, in his case, resulted in agonizing walnut-sized cysts. And there were a lot of mosquitoes in the terrain in which Che and his comrades lived, hid, fought and sometimes died.

That disastrous start to Castro's revolution ought to have spelled the end of the venture. Given an almost complete lack of guns, ammunition, food and other essential supplies, and the unreliability and duplicity of early guides and informants, Castro could have been forgiven if he'd simply walked away from what would appear to have been an obviously doomed enterprise. Far better – and more sensible – to return to Mexico, recoup, regroup and rebuild.

Unbelievably, they decided to press on. Supplementing their few arms – at first, one rifle shared by two or three men – by capturing weapons from government detachments, and later by successfully appealing for supplies from fellow dissidents and supporters in Cuba, they were also boosted by aid and recruits from within Cuba and various South American countries.

There is also strong evidence that some of the guns and ammunition which reached Fidel in later months got through with the compliance of some members of the CIA who were pragmatically playing both ends against the other. They would have known, despite the public blustering of President Dwight D Eisenhower's administration, that Fidel Castro was not – at this stage, at least, and not in the true sense of the word – a communist. A committed Marxist-Leninist, certainly, but if he emerged victorious he could, they hoped with a big maybe, possibly prove malleable, or even bribeable. US intelligence may have been pragmatic, but it was also to prove way off the mark. Quite simply, Fidel Castro's revolution was not for sale.

The initial indifference of Cuba's campesinos, the rural peasants and smallholders, gradually turned to warm appreciation of the rebels' mission. Unlike Batistá's men, who stole from and brutalized the populace, the guerrillas treated people well, while the vision Fidel Castro, Raúl and Che projected of life after victory was a rainbow-hued one of an end to servility and of a more equitable society. And, unlike most of Batistá's troops, who would often put themselves into a fast reverse gear when things got too hot for them, these rebels fought with guts, despite the overwhelming odds.

According to everyone who saw him in action, Che's relationship with the campesinos was, generally, especially good. Like Fidel, he would set up a new administration, with strict but eminently just civil and penal codes, in all those areas he liberated from government control. As well as establishing proper and fair judicial systems, the rebels would also distribute food and levy taxes. As word spread into neighboring areas, peasant support grew, so that the next offensive would start with the advantage of vital, reliable local intelligence and covert aid, not to mention an ever-increasing number of fresh recruits.

During the two long years Castro's revolutionary army spent in Cuba's vast and inhospitable wilderness, Che would prove himself a brilliant tactician and fearless fighter – his eventually published volumes on guerrilla warfare being widely acknowledged as among the most definitive on that particular subject. His growing list of military achievements made his rapid emergence as one of Castro's most trusted military aides and personal confidants inevitable.

ABOVE Valle De Vinales, Cuba – part of the wilderness where Castro and his men spent two long years.

ABOVE Che travelled on horseback whenever his asthma made walking imposssible – at del Escambray in Las Villas.

OPPOSITE The guerrilla leader and his fighters at a secret location near the Cuban coast in 1957. Che is second from the left.

It was not merely a matter of Fidel having a restricted set of options, which he did, of course. Che's early promotion to the rank of platoon commander was justified not only by the overall success and gains made by his detachment, but also the speed and efficiency with which he trained even the greenest of recruits, gaining both their loyalty and affection by making time to listen to their problems and entertaining them during breaks between engagements with readings from the likes of Robert Louis Stevenson, Cervantes, the French short story writer Alphonse Daudet, and inspirational lyric poets such as the Chilean Pablo Neruda. But he was also, as we shall see, a strict disciplinarian.

In time, only too aware of the importance of the written word, Che would use a cumbersome hand-cranked duplicating machine to produce his own 'newspaper' in the field, so helping to boost morale and improve communications. It was this which endeared him to foreign journalists who managed to circumvent the Batistá régime's security forces and visit the guerrillas. If he could overcome the apparently insurmountable hassles of writing and creating a regular newsletter in such conditions, Che was clearly an exceptional man, and one after the intrepid newshounds' own hearts. The fact that he was intelligent, handsome and very articulate also helped to raise his profile in the stream of features and film documentaries which followed such visits. A romantic hero, almost unique in 20th century conflicts, was born.

There was, however, a dark and unforgiving side to Che which the journalists did not see. A martinet who candidly admitted that he once shot a man who had fallen asleep while on guard duty, Che would punish even the slightest infringements with long, public and humiliating tirades, as well as the imposition of severe punishments – extended spells of exhausting night-watch duties or, even worse, a withdrawal of rations from men who were already subsisting on next to nothing.

This was a characteristic which has gained Che Guevara a number of critics through the years, and was one which would appal the French writer, Régis Debray, when he visited Che in Bolivia during his last, ill-fated expedition. Like others who view the Guevara legend through untinted lenses, Debray suggests that Che's absolute, even simplistic, black-and-white fervor never allowed him to be – or, more important, perceived as being – weak in any way. Transgressions or treachery deserved only the most severe reprisals and Che ordered, with no hesitation or sign of regret, the summary execution of a number of men who were revealed as traitors or spies.

Che could never bring himself to apologize for such executions. **'War is harsh,'** he would write later, in *Episodes of the Cuban Revolutionary War*, **'and at a time when the enemy was intensifying its aggressiveness, one could not tolerate even the suspicion of treason.'** With no jails or other types of confinement at their disposal, the guerrillas had no viable option.

The same was true of civilian criminals unlucky enough to fall into their hands. In October 1957, while operating in the Cararacas region, a gang led by a man called Chino Chang was captured by Camilo Cienfuegos. This gang had long terrorized the area, inflicting theft,

ABOVE Commander Che Guevara (of Castro's Column 8) listening to his instruction from HQ via radio.

murder, torture and rape on the population. Worse, they had done so in the name of the revolution.

Chang and another man, an admitted rapist, were sentenced to death. Tied to a tree in the jungle, the two were shot, but not until a delay caused by Chang's request for Father Guillermo Sardiñas – a priest who'd joined the rebels five months earlier and would become a commander – to administer the last rites. As Sardiñas was not in the area, Chang went to his death requesting that his executioners make it known that he had asked for a priest. As Che noted, it was almost as if Chang believed that **'this public testimony would serve as an extenuating circumstance in the heareafter.'**

It was then that the rebels conducted a mock execution of three other young gang members, an event which would form the basis of a Pulitzer Prize-winning feature by US journalist Andrew St George, in *Look* magazine. Although the trio were patently guilty, Fidel Castro felt they had been seduced by Chang and should be given another chance. The boys were blindfolded and shots were fired into the air. When they realized that they'd been spared, their relief and joy was understandably effusive, one of them throwing his arms around Che and planting 'a big noisy kiss' on him in gratitude. Che admiitted this was 'barbaric' but said that although the men did not deserve death, they had committed serious offences. All three men joined the Rebel Army.

There would be long periods when Che would suffer personal agonies because his isolated hiding places made it impossible to get supplies of vital asthma medicines.

He learned to relieve the worst symptoms with a local remedy, smoking the dry leaf of a plant called clarin, but Che's fortitude, his continued success in battle, and his quickly-acquired grasp of tactics all served as testament to his superiority. If he could overcome such obstacles as crippling asthma, poisonous cysts and festering wounds, he was surely entitled to expect nothing less from his men.

As hard, unrelenting and bitter as the rebel campaign was, it was not without its humour, as Che was later keen to remind readers and rapt listeners. Six months into the great adventure, he was asked to make his début as a dentist.

The first extraction (without the benefits of an anaesthetic) was fairly routine, if bloody. However, the second – a canine tooth belonging to a soldier called Joel Iglesias – resisted all of Che's pulling and heaving. It would still be in the man's mouth when the revolutionaries finally marched into Havana eighteen months later. It is reasonable to assume that one of Joel's first objectives then was to find a real dentist who could finish Che's botched job!

The total lack of painkillers, and Che's almost complete inexperience with the kind of drastic emergency surgery he was called on to perform with depressing regularity, often forced him to resort to what he called 'psychological anaesthesia'. 'In plain language', he confessed, 'that means insulting the patients whenever they complained about the pain.'

There was also the matter of hunger, a constant companion – and fixation – for the guerrillas. On one memorable occasion, Che's ragged band arrived at the smallholding of a sympathetic campesino, who made them welcome with the first real food they'd eaten in many days. They were all promptly ill with stomach cramps, having eaten too much too fast, although the one who suffered worst was the group's most corpulent member – a man constantly moaning about the lack of rations. His discomfort was undoubtedly due to his having devoured an entire goat kid on his own!

There is also wry humor in Che's recollection of the time, in the spring of 1957, when he was assigned the task of escorting three American teenagers – Charles Ryan, Victor Buchman and Michael Garney – to a rendezvous with Fidel, where a US journalist, Bob Taber, also waited to interview the youngsters, who were abscondees from the US Navy base at Guantánamo in south-east Cuba (which is there to this day), where their fathers were serving.

While Che could appreciate the international public relations value to the rebels' cause in such a manouevre, he was irked that he was being forced to withdraw himself and his men from what had been a series of profitable (especially in terms of the acquisition of vital arms) encounters with government forces.

Worse, while he didn't doubt their sincerity in joining the guerrillas, the teenagers were physically incapable of keeping up with the back-breaking, energy-sapping pace Che and his men tried to maintain as they headed across country.

Time, and Che's patience, vanished as he was forced to carry out a series of running medical repairs on the boys. Two of them would depart from the Sierra Maestra, with Bob Taber, without having heard a shot fired in anger. The third (not named by Che in his memoirs) would stay on and see action – in May, when the guerrillas took the army garrison in the coastal town of El Uvero. Then he, too, departed, his Latin American adventuring days over.

That brief but bloody battle led to the government taking the remarkably inept decision to close down all such remote and exposed military outposts. While this necessarily reduced the rebels' chances of seizing much-needed arms, ammunition and other military supplies, it opened their way to taking under their control a number of smaller communities without excessive loss and, in so doing, greatly extended their spheres of influence.

El Uvero proved a major turning point in the revolutionary war, raising the guerrilla's morale even though their losses, in terms of both dead and wounded, had been heavy.

Their success sent out a clear signal, to Havana and to the rest of the world, that Castro's revolutionary brigade was capable of inflicting more than just a bloody nose on Batistá's regiments. Even though the El Uvero garrison was relatively small and lightly-defended, Fidel Castro's men had proved their mettle in fine form.

They began to realise that history was, indeed, on their side. It was time to begin building on that success, and start the long and gruelling battles which would eventually culminate with the final triumphant march on the city of Havana in December 1958.

BELOW Castro leads a strategy meeting at the Sierra Maestra base camp II during the final months of the revolution.

revolut

Power and Glory

By the summer of 1958, with support for Castro's ever-growing army spreading like wildfire in Cuba's towns and cities, and the Batistá régime adding fuel to the fire of its eventual destruction with a brutal programme of arrests, torture and worse for suspected Castro sympathisers, Che had been elevated to the rank of commandante, the highest in the revolutionary army and one he shared only with Fidel, Raúl Castro and Juan Almeida. By the end of the year, Delio Gómez Ochoa and Camilo Cienfuegos would join that élite.

Che's rise to the top had been meteoric but was fitting reward for a man who had not only proved himself a born and inspired leader of men, but one who led both by example and from the front. Some of his exploits may have bordered on the reckless, and there may have been occasions when he was fortunate to escape capture or death, but there was no doubt that he had a genius for extracting one more push, one more effort, one more act of bravery from men who could have been forgiven for telling him to go forth and multiply, or words to that effect!

It was this readiness to pitch into the most desperate and apparently unwinnable situations to which Fidel Castro would pay tribute, in October 1967, when he confirmed the news of Che Guevara's death to the people of Cuba.

'And naturally this aroused the highest admiration, and twice the highest admiration, for a fellow combatant fighting alongside us, who had not been born here – a man of profound ideals, a man in whose mind stirred the dream of struggle in other parts of the continent and who was, nonetheless, so altruistic, so disinterested, so willing to do the most difficult things, to constantly risk his life . . . ', Castro told his audience, adding:

'Che was an incomparable soldier. Che was an incomparable leader. Che was, from a military point of view, an extraordinarily capable man, extraordinarily courageous, extraordinarily aggressive. If, as a guerrilla, he had his Achilles' heel, its was this excessively aggressive quality, his resolute contempt for danger.'

In December 1956 Castro's forces had begun to separate and form new, smaller units which could harass and pursue the enemy on a number of fronts. At first, and for what became known as the First Eastern Front, which operated across the Sierra Maestra and Oriente Province, the guerrillas were divided into three Columns – numbered 1, 7 and 31 as a remarkably effective way of tricking enemy commanders into believing that Castro had more men at his disposal than he actually did! It was a simple ruse which they would maintain throughout the progress of the guerilla campaign.

Column 4 – the first main body of men to split away from the First Eastern Front and concentrate solely on the Sierra Maestra region – was given to Che in July 1957. In April 1958 that force would divide again,

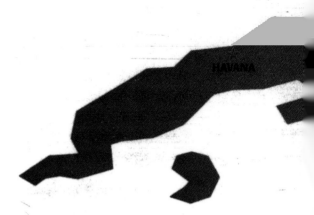

with Che assuming the role of commander of a re-named Column 8, while a newly-established Column 2 was headed by Camilo Cienfuegos.

In March 1958, Raúl Castro (until then leading the original Column 6) was given charge of the Second Eastern Front, which incorporated Columns 6, 16, 17, 18, 19 and 20. At the same time, Juan Almeida – who had headed operations in the Oriente/Santiago de Cuba regions – took control of the Third Eastern Front and Columns 3, 9 and 10.

The Fourth Eastern Front (consisting of Columns 32, 12 and 14!) was launched in October 1958 under the command of Delio Gómez Ochoa, who would eventually unite with Fidel's force (with Columns numbered 13 and 11) to launch the Camagüey and Pinar del Rio Fronts as final victory neared at year's end.

It was in the summer of 1958 that Fidel entrusted Che with the vital, but apparently impossible task of leading two columns (one commanded by Cienfuegos, the other by Che) from the Sierra Maestra to the Escambray Hills in the central province of Las Villas. If that bold move was successful, the rebel army would effectively control pretty much two-thirds of Cuba and present Castro with a formidable advantage when he came to launch his final planned offensive against Batistá in December.

Che's achievement in completing this formidable mission, across 500 kilometres of wilderness and despite having a total of only 230 men at his disposal while the enemy was still numbered in thousands, remains a remarkable *tour de force* in modern warfare. Even more remarkable was the fact that he did it in a mere six weeks, even though there were times when his force was completely surrounded, outnumbered, outgunned and apparently over-run.

There was no doubt in Che's mind as to why he and his men succeeded in penetrating Las Villas Province and capturing their ultimate objective, the strategically crucial city of Santa Clara. His own explanation makes fascinating reading, and could serve as a template for all insurgents:

'The more uncomfortable the guerrilla fighter is, and the more he is initiated into the rigours of nature, the more he feels at home; his morale is higher; his sense of security greater . . . He has learned to risk his life . . . to trust it to luck like a tossed coin . . . It matters little to the individual guerrilla whether or not he survives.'

'The enemy soldier . . . is the junior partner of the dictator; his salary and his pension are worth some suffering and some dangers, but they are never worth his life. If the price of maintaining them will cost it, he is better off giving them up . . . withdrawing from the face of guerrilla danger.'

Withdrawing from danger was never Che's way and there are numerous stories of his bravery under fire, his refusal to take cover when everyone around him was diving into ditches and bushes, even tales of him standing brazenly in the open, a cigar clamped between his teeth as he calmly watched government planes coming in to attack his positions. You can't rush a good cigar!

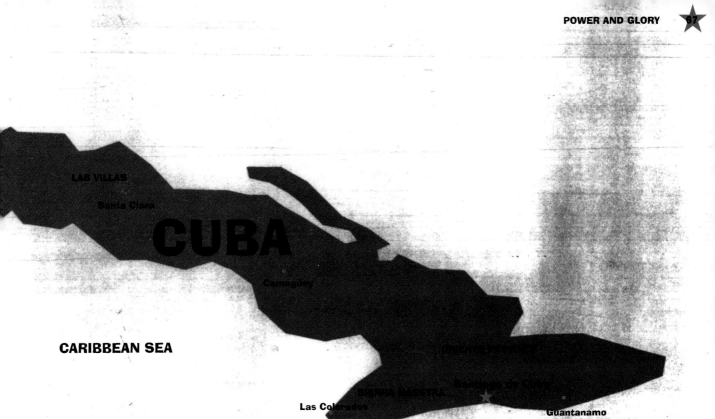

LAS VILLAS

Santa Clara

CUBA

Camaguey

CARIBBEAN SEA

Las Colorados

SIERRA MAESTRA

Santiago de Cuba

Guantanamo

It was during the Las Villas campaign that Che first met, and began to develop a close relationship with, Aleida March de la Torre, a young Cuban woman who'd originally served the rebels as a messenger but had become a full-blown combatant when her activities came to the attention of the secret police in Santa Clara. She was forced to flee for the doubtful but preferable security of Che's camp. In June 1959, when the victory in Cuba had been won and the dust of battle had subsided, Che would negotiate an amicable divorce from Hilda and marry Aleida. They would have four children – Aleida (Aleidita), Camilo, Celia (Celita) and Ernesto (Ernestico, who was only two years old when his father died).

Typically for a man noted for his outstanding charm and courtesy, Che remained good friends with his first wife, who would later move to Cuba with their daughter, Hildita, and take up a post with the Agrarian Reform Institute. Hilda was eventually re-married, to the Cuban painter Miguel Nin Chacon, and died of cancer in February 1974.

All that lay in an unimaginable future. There were still many bloody battles to be fought and won. When Batistá risked all by launching a counter-offensive against Che at Santa Clara in late December – throwing in a huge number of army reservists in a vain last-ditch attempt to save both the Leoncio Vidal garrison (the largest fortress in central Cuba) and the very future of his régime – Che's successful defense of the citadel spelled the end of the line for the dictator, for his military

command, his political power base and for the hundreds of US and Mafia-backed concerns which had dominated Cuban society for so long.

The taking, and holding, of Santa Clara by Che included the demolition and capture of an armoured train packed with anti-aircraft and machine guns, and what he called 'a fabulous quantity of ammunition', a police station (along with two tanks), before he negotiated the surrender of the Leoncio Vidal garrison. Volunteer suicide squads had cleared the way for the main rebel force and it's a measure of the loyalty and commitment which Che attracted among his troops that many more men offered to pitch themselves into battle as part of that kamikaze mission than he actually needed or was prepared to sacrifice.

A final concerted multi-pronged push by Castro's revolutionary army was enough to ensure victory. On New Year's Day, 1959, Fulgencio Batistá fled Havana for a life of exile in the Dominican Republic, handing over military power to General Eulogio Cantillo and the presidency to Dr Manuel Urrutia. Refusing to recognize this new régime, Fidel called for a nationwide general strike the next day to paralyze the country. In the face of a 'surrender or die' ultimatum from Fidel, government forces in the army garrison of Santiago de Cuba – long since isolated behind rebel lines on the south-eastern coast – laid down their arms that afternoon.

Within 24 hours the columns led by Che and Camilo Cienfuegos had reached Havana, where they took control of the capital's main army bases, Camp Columbia and La Cabaña. As the streets of Havana filled with celebrating citizens, and while rebel supporters helped quell the last significant pockets of resistance, Fidel Castro entered Havana at the head of a large force on January 8. The war had been won. The greater battle – to rebuild Cuba as a socialist Utopia – could begin in earnest. And Che Guevara was determined to play as active a role in that task as he had during the two years of brutal fighting in the Sierra Maestra.

BELOW and OPPOSITE Thousands celebrated the end of the Batistà regime as the victorious rebel army entered Havana.

Building a Dream

The country of which Fidel Castro found himself appointed prime minister on February 16, 1959 presented him with a daunting set of problems, the solutions to which would not be achieved easily or quickly, if ever. It is worth outlining something of the history which had caused those problems.

The largest island in the West Indies (almost 1,100 km long and an average 80 km wide), Cuba lies some 120 km south of Florida and 300 km due east of Mexico's Yucatan Peninsula. Originally colonized by the Spanish in the 16th century, the indigenous population of Cuba had been almost wiped out within 100 years, forcing the colonists to import black African slaves to work the mines and plantations they'd established. The plantations grew either tobacco or sugar cane, both of which thrived in Cuba's dark fertile soil and sub-tropical climate, while the wealth of nickel, copper, salt, cobalt and other minerals guaranteed almost limitless prosperity for mine owners.

Constantly beleaguered by pirates and the navies of rival powers, Cuba's colonists resolutely disregarded Spanish government restrictions on commercial trade with neighbour nations or foreign companies and earned themselves a formidable reputation as smugglers and black marketeers. In 1763, after a seven-year war with the British (who actually captured Havana at one stage), Madrid relaxed those restrictions, encouraging the expansion of trade, further colonization and the development of Cuba's vast agricultural potential. As a result, Cuba's population had increased to more than 550,000 by 1817, at which time all remaining trade limitations were eliminated.

However, the colonists chafed at what they viewed as continued Spanish repression, and Cuba was torn by revolts and bids for independence for much of the rest of the century. In 1844, a slave uprising was suppressed with ruthless brutality by Spanish forces and, in 1851, a popular movement to annex the island to the United States ended with the capture and execution of its leader. That annexation scheme found favour with successive US administrations, although repeated offers to buy the island were firmly rejected by Madrid. In 1868, a declaration of independence by Carlos Manuel de Céspedes led to a bloody and costly ten-year war which ended only when Spain granted the Cuban rebels many important political concessions.

Slavery was abolished in Cuba in 1886, while the importation of cheap Chinese labour ended five years later. In a rare display of pragmatic wisdom, Spain decreed equal civil status for Cuba's black and white populations in 1893. It was not enough, however, and in 1895 the Cuban revolution resumed under the leadership of General Máximo Gómez y Báez and the writer-patriot José Martí. Three years later the United States intervened, its support for the rebels precipitated by the sinking, in Havana Harbour, of the battleship *Maine* by a mysterious explosion and the hysteria created and fanned by William Randolph Hearst's populist *Morning Journal* newspaper in New York.

ABOVE Major General Maximo Gomez – Commander in Chief of the Cuban Army Of Liberation.

om *Kladderadatsch.*]   [December 30, 1894.

The Spanish-American War would last a mere six months, after
which Spain relinquished all claims on Cuba and an American military
government was installed to rule the island until 1902, when the Cuban
Republic was formalized by the election of its first president, Tomas
Estrada Palma. The new constitution, however, incorporated provisions
not only for a US military and naval presence on the island in perpetuity,
but conditions for American military intervention in the future.

With such sweeping safeguards as their security, it was inevitable that
entrepreneurial US corporations – as well as less legitimate elements –
would begin investing heavily in Cuba. The seeds of discontent were
sown and a harvest of unrest, rebellion and outrage would soon follow,
resulting in numerous nationalist revolts, all of which were put down
with varying degrees of severity.

By the end of World War I, US domination of Cuba's agricultural,
industrial and financial affairs was almost total. Elected to the presidency
in 1924 on a platform of liberal reforms, Gerardo Machado y Morales
swiftly wrecked the urban economy further via huge borrowings, adopted
dictatorial powers to gain a second term in office and became a tyrannical
despot. He was overthrown by a military-backed *coup d'état* in 1933, but
not even the Cuban army was able to cope with the numerous periods
of unrest and violence which followed and which were only calmed, in
1936, by the election of Federico Laredo Brú, a former soldier who
was backed by the then leader of the Cuban Senate, Fulgencio Batistá.

All the while, US business domination of Cuba's natural resources was
being supplemented by growing investment in the island by American
crime syndicates. During Prohibition in the 1920s and early '30s, the

ABOVE "Only a little step and Uncle Sam will be in Cuba."
A caption on a cartoon from *Kladderadatsch*,
December 30, 1894.

ABOVE Officers of the Cuban Cavalry – approximately 10,000 men took part in a military review before President Iaredo Bru and Colonel Batista on 24 February 1944.

proximity to the US mainland of a tropical paradise, with local politicians only too happy to be bribed into compliance and complicity, made Cuba a natural and easy target for the Mafia. Hotels, holiday complexes, brothels and brewing concerns abounded, with civic leaders and police safely – and openly – on their payrolls.

Brú's introduction of economic and social reforms helped ease tension, as did the drafting of a new constitution in 1940, the year Fulgencio Batistá first succeeded to the presidency. In 1944 he was replaced by Ramón Grau San Martín, head of a broad coalition, and although his first year of office was marked by severe food shortages, San Martín was able to recover his popularity in 1945 by negotiating an increase in the price of sugar with the American government led by Franklin D. Roosevelt.

Fluctuating world prices in that commodity – Cuba's single biggest export product – meant that Grau San Martín had to cope with a series of financial crises, many of which triggered further civil unrest which was exacerbated by the Cuban people's awareness of the graft and greed of successive administrations and the fact that their island had become little more than one of Uncle Sam's playthings.

Grau San Martín was succeeded as president by Carlos Prío Socarrás in 1948, and although he cut retail prices by 10 per cent in a bid to halt rampant inflation, the cost of living continued to rise, as did various dissident groups. In March 1952, former President Batistá seized power with the support of the military, suspended the constitution, dissolved Congress and promised democratic elections the next year. That promise was broken when Batistá was confronted by an uprising in Oriente Province, led by a young lawyer called Fidel Castro, a member of the Cuban People's Party.

With the rebellion crushed and Castro sentenced to 15 years in jail, Batistá finally called those long-promised elections in 1954. His only opponent, Grau San Martín, withdrew at the last moment claiming (with every justification) that his supporters were being terrorized, and Batistá was re-elected. In February 1955, Batistá foolishly celebrated his inauguration by announcing a widespread amnesty for many of his country's prisoners. One of those he released was Fidel Castro, who left for enforced exile in the United States before joining his July 26 comrades in Mexico. It was to prove the single most expensive mistake Batistá could have made.

To be fair to him, Fulgencio Batistá's second period of power signalled the introduction of an economic development programme which happily coincided with a period of relative stability in world sugar prices. However, most of the population continued to live near or below the poverty line and there was little or no prospect of real change, nor of greater improvement so long as Cuba's agricultural and industrial bases were owned by US conglomerates, and while the administration was almost entirely 'owned' by US criminal institutions.

It was this legacy – and his determination to transform Cuban society – which had driven Fidel Castro and would continue to dictate his decisions in coming years. That determination was shared by Che Guevara who, while neither a Cuban nor a Communist Party member, knew he would never have a better chance to put his Marxist-Leninist ideals into action.

The first role Castro gave Che was that of commander of Havana's La Cabaña fortress, effectively making him head of the military. On January 9, 1959, the newly-formed Cuban Council of Ministers paid Che the signal honor of making him a full citizen of Cuba, at which time he took the opportunity to legalize his nickname. In one stroke Ernesto became Che and Che became a household name around the world.

There was an early disillusionment in store, however, and one which struck Che so forcibly he would recount it many times in later years as a warning to others who aspired to create a revolution. Among those who had joined Fidel's cause at a relatively late stage were former Cuban army officers whose true loyalty and motives Che had always suspected. Chief among these were Gutiérrez Menoyo and his inseparable lieutenant, Fleitas, who had led the 2nd National Front military unit at Escambray, and were now temporarily ensconced in Havana's smart Hotel Capri.

While their principal task was supposed to be securing the city's most strategically important positions in case of counter-attack from the few

BELOW Peasant children far from the Cuban capital. Their homes in the background show the extent of the poverty.

forces which remained loyal to Batistá, Menoyo, Fleitas and their hangers-on managed to run up a bar and food bill of $15,000 in only a few days – probably close to $100,000 in today's values. To Che, this was both an appalling dereliction of duty and abuse of privilege.

Many key posts were awarded to career professionals who had elected to stay in Cuba, and while some sensitive jobs were given to the likes of Menoyo, Fleitas and their ilk, supervision and surveillance of them was to prove very strict, as was the punishment meted out to those who succumbed to temptation. They might betray the revolution, but they would not be allowed to get away with such treachery.

Interestingly, while Che's long-held and ongoing suspicion of the Communist Party still seemed apparent, it was he who would persuade a reluctant Fidel to appoint communists to many strategic positions in the areas of planning and administration. There can be little doubt that Che believed that they had the 'purity' of idealism necessary to create the socialist state he wanted to help create in Cuba.

With thousands of Batistá's cohorts having joined him in flight, one of Castro's earliest priorities was to capture and punish the most notorious members and supporters of the old régime who had not managed to escape. A series of heavily-publicized trials were held, and more than 500 of those convicted were executed for crimes against the people. Che acted as chairman at many of those hearings, handing out death sentences as readily and unemotionally as he had done in the Sierra Maestra or Las Villas.

It was Che who initiated the harsh prison work-camps into which many more of the old guard would be consigned, but did not approve their introduction as part of the new, tough-line penal process until he had personally experienced the regimen they would impose on inmates. Satisfied that it was hard but fair, Che signed the authorization order.

Of equal importance, however, was the need to set the major revolutionary reforms in motion which Castro did, on May 17, by nationalizing all Cuban land. The campesinos no longer had landlords to oppress them – as members of a socialist state they became their own landlords at a stroke. A limit of 30 caballeriás, about 1,000 acres, was set on individual land-holdings – a move which effectively stripped some $850 million worth of property from US agricultural interests and prompted President Dwight D Eisenhower once more to describe Fidel as 'a dangerous communist'.

Aware that US hostility was certain only to worsen, Castro travelled to Washington in April 1959, 'enjoyed' a two-hour meeting with Vice-President Richard Nixon, addressed key figures from the newspaper, magazine and broadcast media, was allowed to plead the new Cuba's case to the General Assembly of the United Nations in New York and attracted an enthusiastic crowd of more than 30,000 when he addressed a rally in Central Park.

Castro was only too aware that while the Eisenhower administration had so far stayed its hand, his intended confiscation and nationalization of all US assets in Cuba meant that his country's single biggest customer – some 75 per cent of all Cuban agricultural and industrial products

RIGHT Fidel Castro at the United Nations in New York. This lightning trip was a public relations triumph which climaxed with a rally for 30,000 in Central Park – September 1960

went to the United States – would inevitably slam the door firmly in his face. There was the very real prospect of a US-led worldwide embargo on all trade with Cuba. He had to find new markets quickly, and forge new alliances to help bankroll his revolution.

There was only one man Fidel was confident in entrusting with this crucial mission. In June 1959 Che began what would become a lightning world tour of socialist states, visiting the Soviet Union, Europe, Africa, China, Japan and South America to state Fidel's case in person. In most countries his arrival was greeted with applause and acclaim, with his heavily-emphasized guerrilla battle exploits lending weight to his status as a true revolutionary hero.

When Che returned to Havana in September, he had not only secured the all-important financial and political support of both the communist super-powers, the Soviet Union and China, but he had also opened the way for what would be fruitful negotiations with a dozen other countries around the world only too willing to buy Cuban goods, whether it be sugar, tobacco, ores or minerals.

It was a formidable achievement, and one which would be matched in that first year only by his vision on the matter of Cuba's international financial reserves. While Che had been appointed chief of the Industrial Department at an October meeting of the National Institute of Agrarian Reform (INRA) – the key group charged with transforming Cuba's creaking rural production systems – on November 26 he was also appointed as head of the National Bank of Cuba, whose bank notes he would make internationally famous by using the simple, informal signature 'Che'.

At his first meeting with the bank's board, Che asked a deceptively simple question which no one had apparently considered before: where were Cuba's gold reserves actually stored? When he learned that they were mostly in the US Treasury's vaults, in Fort Knox, Kentucky, Che ordered that they be sold on the international bullion market and converted into hard cash currencies which could then be held in Swiss and Canadian bank accounts, far out of Uncle Sam's reach. When, early in 1960, the US government froze all of Cuba's American-based assets, it was seen that Che's bold move had saved the country from bankruptcy. Not bad for a man with no economics training to his credit, but typical of a man who had been well-schooled in the craft of second-guessing the opposition.

Che's dedication to making the revolution work was, by all accounts, every bit as complete as his tirelessness in war had been, or his readiness to study as a young man crippled by asthma. Holding down two highly important government posts, he was known to work for as long as thirty-six hours at a stretch, calling meetings after midnight and eating on the run. Che invariably refused to take a break for meals. 'Business lunches take too much time,' he once explained. 'Anyway, you can't talk with food in your mouth!' He also worked as a volunteer in mines, factories and sugarcane fields, his presence good for morale among the workforce.

Castro was aware that Che was a superb and inspirational public speaker and, despite his lieutenant's genuine reluctance to step into the limelight, would press him into service whenever he could. Like Castro,

LEFT Havana 1961 – Che was now Major Ernesto 'Che' Guevara, President of the Cuban National Bank and a powerful figure in Castro's regime.

BELOW A bare chested Che helps with a public housing construction project near Havana, 1962

Che continued to dress in combat fatigues with black paratroop boots and beret. Strikingly handsome and an idol to all who had heard the legends of his war exploits, Che's appearances at factories and plants were guaranteed to create excitement, while his words were calculated to drive home messages vital to Cuba's economic survival.

With all American-owned companies nationalized by Castro – who had finally abandoned false modesty and accepted the post of President temporarily held by Batistá's nominee, Dr Manuel Urrutia – it was absolutely vital that those appointed to run the country's industries should understand that they really were in charge. Quotas and targets might be set in Havana, but it was the new managers' responsibility to ensure that they were met or exceeded. There were no American bosses to give the orders any more – results and progress were entirely dependent on the Cuban people using their own initiative.

Che's oratory was, by all accounts, formidable, if somewhat overblown and overlong on formal occasions. He could cajole, bully, amuse or enthral his worker audiences with a disarming and charming confidentiality which managed never to be patronizing. He was truly just 'one of them', and even if some of his political rhetoric and more arcane theoretical references went over their heads, his listeners responded with increased effort and productivity.

Only so far, however. When Che insisted on centralizing Cuba's industrial and agricultural management structures and rejected workers' calls for wage increases linked to increased productivity – advising them that public acclaim for exceeding targets should be reward enough – he learned that the workforce, sadly, believed that there was more to life than medals, certificates and pats on the back. None of those things paid the rent, purchased food or improved their general lot. Productivity began to flag, then sink as low worker morale and antiquated, irreplaceable machinery combined to end that part of Che's dream, as did the American trade ban which starved Cuba of the essential raw materials and industrial equipment which was vital to the nation's survival and economic success.

And, all the while, there was more travelling to be done. In 1960, apart from tackling his domestic political duties, Che was to be found in Czechoslovakia, the Soviet Union, China and North Korea, all of whose leaders he persuaded to commit themselves to further commercial agreements as Cuba's international trade lifelines were cut by the US and its Western partners.

Complex swap deals had to be arranged, dummy import-export companies set up all over the world, to move embargoed Cuban produce from one place to another and bring in vital imports of raw materials and cash. The operation was often labyrinthine and, as such, was open to outright theft and punitive middleman fees, but it worked to a more or less acceptable degree. Cuba may have been isolated, but it was never completely cut off from world markets. The profit motive saw to that.

In 1961 Che was appointed Minister of Industry, as well as briefly resuming military duties to take part in the operation to repel the Bahiá de los Cochinos (Bay of Pigs) invasion launched, on April 17, by a group of pro-Batistá, CIA-trained Cuban exiles with the newly incumbent President John F Kennedy's less than fulsome blessing.

Of the 1300 or so insurgents who landed on Cuba's southern coast without the US Air Force support which Kennedy refused to authorize – and with which they could perhaps have succeeded in creating a positive foothold on the island – 90 were killed and the rest captured by Cuban revolutionary forces. They would be held for close on a year until ransomed by wealthy Cuban exiles – albeit with covert CIA financial support – for an estimated $53 million in food and medicines. It was the sweetest of victories.

President Kennedy would have his revenge, however, in the fateful October of 1962. When Castro secretly agreed to allow the Soviet Union to site nuclear missiles on Cuban soil, and thus create a nuclear strike-force capability on America's doorstep, the US President ordered a military blockade of the island on October 22, and in doing so confronted Soviet leader Nikita Khrushchev with a blood-chilling ultimatum: turn back the ships – which American reconnaissance aircraft had proved were carrying missiles – and dismantle the silos already established on Cuba, or break the blockade which would effectively press the button to begin a nuclear war. It was a supreme act of brinkmanship, and one which had the world on the edge of its seat as the clock ticked inexorably towards Kennedy's zero-hour. The world has never, before or since, been nearer to all-out nuclear war.

Khrushchev backed down on October 28, and Castro, although privately furious with the Soviet leader for repatriating the missiles without consulting him, and at being excluded from the exchanges

BELOW Photographs taken by US surveillance aircraft proved that Soviet missiles were on their way to Cuba, less than 100 miles from the Florida coast.

MISSILE TRANSPORTERS

12 PROB GUIDELINE MISSILES

HEAVY EQUIPMENT

5 MISSILE DOLLIES

20' LONG CYLINDRICAL

MISSILE T

OPEN STORAGE

ABOVE A medium range ballistic missile base in Cuba, along with launchers and other equipment. These pictures were the evidence used by President Kennedy to order his blockade of the island.

between Kennedy and Khrushchev, was all public hugs and smiles when he visited Moscow shortly afterwards.

While there the Cuban leader extracted a financial support package which was to ensure that Cuba would be well subsidised until the Soviet Union finally imploded and collapsed in the early 1990s.

In so doing, however, he managed to alienate the régime in mainland China, which had for long been at ideological loggerheads with the USSR, and therby put himself in a bad light with the other members of the Chinese Bloc.

For his part, Che was even angrier than his leader and friend, never having trusted or liked Khrushchev on either a personal or political level. To him, the Cuban missile crisis was proof positive that the Soviet Union could be an unreliable, untrustworthy mammoth which had shown its true colours back in October 1956 when the Red Army crushed the Hungarian people's attempt to form their own autonomous, more liberal government free from Moscow's control. This was an intervention that was in many ways, Che felt, as imperialistic as any that the American government and CIA had engineered to install or support repressive régimes in South America.

With his seriously jaundiced eyes ever open, Che continued to immerse himself in domestic and international tasks.

What little spare time he did allow himself was spent mainly at home with Aleida, who was now working for the Cuban Federation of Women while helping him expand his family. She also encouraged him to explore classical music, which he had come to love, with Beethoven becoming an especial favourite.

As ever, he was an avid reader. He also maintained a preference for fairly simple food – a typical Che dinner would be steak and salad, accompanied by a glass or two of Spanish brandy.

He continued to favour maté above other drinks – arranging for supplies to be imported clandestinely from the South American mainland – and enjoyed the satisfaction of one of Cuba's finest products, a Monte Cristo No 4 cigar.

Despite all that had been achieved, Che nevertheless chafed at what he perceived as being the relatively slow progress of change in Cuba. Still very much the hard-nosed idealist, he was irked by Fidel Castro's more pragmatic approach to social reform, which invariably involved a certain degree of compromise.

Che's revolutionary dream did not include any margin for compromise and he was soon to make a number of important enemies both at home and abroad, where his criticisms of the major world powers eventually managed to unite the American and Soviet empires against him, along with many local communist parties.

It was that aspect which would sow the seeds of his undoing, and ultimately seal his fate when he embarked on his last great adventure in the jungles of Bolivia.

ABOVE Castro with Soviet leader Nikita Khruschev. Although a crucial ally to Cuba, Khruschev was not a man Che ever liked or completely trusted.

TRI X PAN

International Superstar

Che continued to travel as Castro's envoy and publicist, however, his fervour undimmed, his oratory undiminished in its potency. All the while, his public profile – and what marketing men like to call 'recognition factor' – continued to rise worldwide. Che's presence at a major conference was guaranteed to attract huge crowds eager to catch a glimpse of this derring-do hero, even if his cavalier disregard for democratic niceties could make his more sensitive and less courageous hosts cringe as he strode to the podium, a large sheaf of explosive speech-notes in his hand.

In August 1961, for example, a conference of the Inter-American Economic and Social Council of the Organization of American States (OAS) held in Punta del Este, Uruguay, was graced by the presence of Douglas Dillon, the US Secretary of the Treasury. As the principal paymaster to many of the countries present, Dillon was therefore a main player on that particular stage. He had come to try to bury Cuba with a policy of isolationism, and definitely not to encourage its continued membership of the OAS.

Among the crowd of reporters waiting at Montevideo's Carrasco International Airport, and covering the conference for *The New York Times*, was the political journalist John Gerassi. As he so ably later described in his 1968 volume, *Venceremos! The Speeches and Writings of Che Guevara*, Gerassi witnessed the full force and magnetism of Che Guevara's popularity and appeal.

Like many who had the opportunity to meet Che in person and share many long hours of invariably heated debate on world affairs, Gerassi encountered a charismatic figure with an almost mesmeric gaze. It was the same gaze which had calmed a terrified Silvio Lozano at the San

BELOW and RIGHT A formidable public speaker, Che's appearances on the world stages only increased his fame and reputation.

'Cuba is part of a world that is under anguishing tension . . . it does not know if one of the parties . . . will commit the clumsy blunder of unleashing a conflict that will necessarily be atomic. And Cuba is watchful . . . because it knows that imperialism will succumb, wrapped in flames; but it knows that Cuba would also pay, with its blood the price of the defeat of imperialism, and it hopes that this defeat may be achieved by other means . . . and they will not have to pay . . . with the lives of millions of human beings destroyed by atomic fallout.'

Pablo leper colony eight years earlier and would be noted by other more urbane observers through the years, even those not persuaded by the weight of his arguments.

Gerassi also discovered a keen observer who was 'extremely intense and in a great hurry. He gave us the impression that he was convinced that he would soon die and that he must accomplish everything he can as fast as possible'. Gerassi's characterization was that of an extremely dedicated, honest and human person, 'though he had a distance, perhaps even a shyness, which made those qualities difficult to perceive.'

Gerassi was convinced of one thing especially: '. . . that he was not a communist in most of the traditional senses of the word. He believed in a socialist economy. He believed in Socialist Man. He was convinced that these two goals can be achieved . . . and was dedicated to working for their realization without taking orders from any foreign power. He only felt scorn for those who took such orders.'

Before he led the Cuban delegation into abstaining in the final vote to ratify a US motion proposing a new OAS Alliance for Progress, Che spelled out his view of the real state of the world in August 1961 to the Punta del Este conference:

'The world situation is tense . . . The Soviet Union has reaffirmed its decision to sign a German peace treaty, and President Kennedy has announced that he would even go to war over Berlin . . . There is Laos, and the Congo, where Lumumba was murdered by imperialism; there is divided Vietnam and divided Korea; Formosa in the hands of Chiang Kai-shek's gang; there is Argentina, prostrate, and now they want to divide it too; and Tunisia, whose people the other day were machine-gunned for committing the 'crime' of wanting to recover their territory.'

Che's long and often masterful speech, which outlined progress in Cuba since the revolution and defended Castro's decision to allow the Soviet Union to locate troops on the island (Kennedy's promises of non-aggression having been revealed as hollow by the Bay of Pigs invasion, along with attacks on Cuban military airfields by exiled former Batistá régime pilots), ended with a dire warning to the OAS delegates. While he pledged that Cuba itself would not attempt to export its revolution to other parts of the world, he could not assure them that the philosophy and example of the Cuban experience would not be adopted in other South American states.

By April 1967, Che's promise of Cuban non-intervention in the internal affairs of fellow OAS members had long been proved as empty as any made by the arch-enemy's successive presidents, John Kennedy and Lyndon Johnson, regarding Vietnam. He had made inflammatory anti-American and pro-direct action speeches at a number of major international conferences, all of them widely reported and most of them causing often severe embarrassment to his hosts who, in the main, would have preferred to present a more rational and conciliatory image of themselves to the world. Che's tirades merely fuelled the West's propaganda machine, helping the United States and its allies to argue that the Red Menace was alive and well.

BELOW Che listens intently at a session of the General Assembly of the United Nations via the translator.

It was during that month, when Che was firmly esconsed in Bolivia, that his fiercest attack on US imperialism – and his most fervent call for international revolution – was published. It came in the form of a pamphlet published in Havana under the title *Message to the Tricontinental: Create two, three . . . many Vietnams.*

After querying the popularly accepted 'fact' that some 21 years had passed since the last world conflagration, Che listed the major international conflicts which made this period of 'peace' questionable – citing Korea and Vietnam as principal examples of arenas in which peace was glaringly absent before listing the rest of Indo-China, the former Belgian Congo, Rhodesia, Bolivia, Guatemala, Colombia, Peru and Venezuela as locations in which Western (mostly US) backed régimes were finding themselves locked in battle with revolutionary forces.

In South America especially Che predicted that the struggle would eventually achieve continental proportions and 'shall be the scene of many great battles fought for the liberation of humanity'.

'It is the road of Vietnam', he averred, '[South] America, a forgotten continent in the last liberation struggles, is now beginning to make itself heard through the Tricontinental as, in the voice of the vanguard of its peoples, the Cuban Revolution will today have a task of much greater relevance: creating a second or a third Vietnam – or the second and third Vietnam of the world.

' . . . imperialism . . . must be defeated in a world confrontation . . . Our share, the responsibility of the exploited and underdeveloped of the world, is to eliminate the foundations of imperialism; our oppressed nations, from where they extract capitals, raw materials, technicians and cheap labour, and to which they export . . . instruments of domination – arms and all kinds of articles, thus submerging us in an absolute dependence.'

The battle to eliminate imperialism would, Che conceded, be long and bloody. But it could be won if the great lesson of the invincibility of the Vietnamese guerrillas took root, and in that context he called on 'the dispossessed masses' and galvanized them into preparation for even more violent repressions.

In a chilling coda, Che spelled out his own credo when he identified hatred as an imperative – 'a relentless hatred of the enemy, impelling us over and beyond the natural limitations that man is heir to and transforming him into an effective, violent, selective and cold killing machine. Our soldiers must be thus; a people without hatred cannot vanquish a brutal enemy.'

If that was Che's true philosophy – and his vehemence suggests it was – it goes a long way to explaining his decision, in 1965, to leave the relative calm of Cuba, his young family and the comfort of his state accomodation, and pitch himself, once more, into the danger of battles which could claim his life.

Che had always maintained close links with the active revolutionary movements of other nations, encouraging the establishing of guerrilla

ABOVE Che stops in Paris to see a show of the Cuban National Ballet on his way to Algiers – April 1964.

ABOVE President Janio Quadros of Brazil decorating Che Guevara in 1961.

training facilities in Cuba for would-be insurgents which could also be used by Cuban military personnel selected to work covertly alongside foreign revolutionary groups. He was painfully aware that a number of fronts had been opened around the world and yearned to become personally involved again.

In Palestine, Abu Jihad and Yasir Arafat's Al-Fatah movement was beginning to make its presence felt in its war with Israel; in Mozambique Eduardo Mondlane's Frelimo guerrillas were beginning to hit the colonial powers; Aghostino Neto's MPLA was flexing its muscles in Angola; renewed and reinvigorated movement could be detected in Peru, Bolivia, Brazil and Venezuela; while in the former Belgian Congo, rebels led by Gaston Soumaliot, Pierre Mulele and Nicholas Olenga were on the march against the puppet régime of Moise Tshombe.

It was this last-named struggle which increasingly attracted Che's interest and loyalties, and one which he was determined to champion wherever, and whenever, he had the opportunity, viewing it as the one which could perhaps unify the Tricontinental into direct action.

In December 1964, for instance, he addressed the General Assembly of the United Nations in New York, and eloquently attacked the recent use of Belgian army forces to recapture the Congo city of Stanleyville (now called Kisangani) when it was seized by rebels loyal to the independence movement begun by Patrice Lumumba, the newly-independent country's first prime minister who was murdered by Tshombe's white mercenary troops in 1961.

'Who were the perpetrators?' he demanded angrily, answering: 'Belgian paratroopers, transported by United States aircraft, which took off from British bases. All free men throughout the world must now make ready to avenge the Congo crime.' If political commentators and Western intelligence services put this last statement down to a routine display of Guevara machismo for the benefit of the world's media, then they were gravely mistaken.

The strongest hint of Che's intention to once more become a guerrilla came in February 1965, in a speech he delivered to an Afro-Asian Solidarity Conference held in Algiers and in which he pinned his colours firmly to the mast of a concerted international fight to end imperialism once and for all. It was an impassioned call for all socialist states to combine resources once that victory had been achieved.

Although he paid lip-service to the aid Cuba had received from the Soviet Union, his implicit criticism of Moscow's reluctance to offer such aid unconditionally was to sever his own few links with the Soviet communist apparatus and cause something of a schism between those who agreed with him and others who thought he had gone one step too far. But there was a great deal to his view that there should be no talk of developing 'mutually profitable trade' when selling raw materials and machinery at world market prices 'cost the backward countries sweat and unlimited suffering'.

During that speech Che also referred specifically to the 'American imperialist attacks' on Vietnam and the Congo which, he said 'must be answered with the supplying of these sister countries with all the weapons of defence they need and with the offer of our complete and absolutely unconditional solidarity.'

After making secret fact-finding trips to a number of African locations – including Mali, Senegal, Ghana, Tanzania – and Egypt, where he told President Gamal Nasser that he intended to give the Congolese rebels his full personal support, he persuaded Fidel Castro to finance a Cuban guerrilla force in readiness for an expedition to Africa.

According to Mohammed Heikel, Nasser's journalist son-in-law, the Egyptian president was astonished when Che said he believed **'we can hurt the imperialists at the core of their interests in Katanga.'** Nasser warned Che against becoming

'another Tarzan, a white man among black men, leading them and protecting them . . . '

and shook his head. 'It can't be done,' he predicted.

Che Guevara was not listening. He had the scent of a new revolution in his nostrils. It was time to move on.

He flew to Beijing where he met Chou En-lai and Chairman Mao Tse-tung. Although the Chinese had distanced themselves from Fidel Castro after he appeared to rely exclusively on Moscow for support, and were still disillusioned by what they perceived as Cuba's reluctance to help draw the Latin-American communist parties into a union with Beijing, Che's internationalist intentions met with their approval and blessing.

Che flew back to Havana on March 14, 1965, to be greeted at the airport by Fidel Castro. Then, as far as the outside world was concerned, he disappeared completely from public view. The next time Che Guevara was seen was in October 1967, when his bullet-riddled body was put on display in Vallegrande.

BELOW LEFT Meeting Chinese leader Chairman Mao Tse Tung during the diplomatic mission to Peking.

BELOW As Minister of Industries, Che heads the Cuban delegation at the United Nations Trade Conference in Geneva in April 1965.

ABOVE November 1960, Che is greeted on landing in the
Chinese capital by a welcoming party that includes the Vice-
Prime Minister Li Hsien-Nien (left) and the obligatory guard
of honour of smiling young women.

CHINA

5 3 gu

Che's Lost Year

It is almost impossible to think of a more complex and insoluble set of intrigue-ridden military and political scenarios than those which were tearing the former Belgian Congo apart in the first half of the 1960s.

A colonial property of the Belgian government since 1908 (and the personal fiefdom of the Belgian royal family for 17 years before that), the new Democratic Republic of the Congo had been granted independence in June 1960 when the landslide victory of Patrice Lumumba's Congolese National Movement (MNC) in Belgian-sponsored elections late in 1959 forced a reluctant Brussels to face reality.

In new elections held in May 1960, the MNC came out so far ahead of the other many parties – most of them established solely to promote traditional tribal interests – that the Belgians' designated president, Joseph Kasavubu, was forced to invite Lumumba to form the republic's first government. A few days after he did this, a rebellion among some army units was followed by a declaration of break-away independence by the mineral-rich province of Katanga. The arrival of Belgian troops in Katanga was officially stated to be a move to ensure the safety of Belgian nationals, but the real objective was soon proved to be their support of the secessionist leader, Moise Tshombe, and the protection of their mineral mining interests.

Despite the arrival of UN troops (as a lamentably inept peace-keeping force), Tshombe's revolt continued and the Belgian troops stayed in place. Lumumba appealed to the Soviet Union for aircraft to transport his troops to Katanga. This, and his invitation to the leaders of other independent African states to meet in the Congo capital, Léopoldville (now Kinshasa), alarmed the West and President Kasavubu. On September 5 he dismissed Lumumba and nine days later was given the support of Joseph Mobutu, then a Congolese army colonel.

In October the UN General Assembly recognized the Kasavubu / Mobutu régime and, shortly thereafter, Lumumba tried to flee Léopoldville for Stanleyville, where his main supporters had control. Captured by Mobutu's troops, Lumumba was handed over to Tshombe's Katanga rebels and murdered in January 1961, his death causing an outcry across Africa and the rest of the world.

With Mobutu now commander-in-chief of the Congolese army, Moise Tshombe was rewarded for his complicity in the murder of Lumumba by a forceful United Nations intervention in Katanga in January 1963. He fled to an exile in Spain, but in 1964 was invited back by Kasavubu, ostensibly to become prime minister and help suppress a rebellion in the eastern Congo.

One of Tshombe's first moves was to request – and receive – the support of both the United States and South Africa's apartheid régime, and to hire white mercenaries commanded by the former British paratroop major, 'Mad' Mike Hoare, a man he had first employed to keep order when he seized Katanga in 1960. In all, a thousand South African and Rhodesian mercenaries were recruited, while the US supplied a number of combat aircraft, ironically piloted by Cuban exiles who had a lot of time on their hands since the Bay of Pigs fiasco.

Massed against them – under the umbrella of a socialist opposition coalition known as the National Liberation Council (NLC), which had been created in October 1963 and was originally based in Brazzaville, capital of the neighboring former French colony of Congo-Brazzaville – were three separate and clearly definable groups.

The first-formed was led by Pierre Mulele – Patrice Lumumba's minister of education and one-time Congo ambassador in Cairo – which started operations in September 1963, in the province of Kwilu, east of Léopoldville. With the support of the Chinese government in Beijing, Mulele's attacks on industrial plants, government administration posts and all members of what his manifesto called the 'exploitating class' began seriously in January 1964.

The second front also came from the east, in the form of a revolt based in Bukumbura, capital of neighboring Burundi. Led by Gaston Soumaliot, one of whose most trusted lieutenants was the former Katangan assembly member Laurent Kabila, this group (also given the tacit support of Beijing) began operations in February 1964, concentrating its activities in the Uvira region of central Kivu, along the Burundi border. (For over 30 years active in the field, Kabila led the rebel alliance which eventually ousted President Mobutu in May 1997).

By June, Soumaliot's rebels – mostly members of the Babembe tribe – had seized the town of Albertville (now Kalemie) on the western shore of Lake Tanganyika. Although Soumaliot intended to use Albertville as the seat of his provisional government, Tshombe's troops and Mike Hoare's mercenaries limited his tenure of Albertville to a few weeks and he'd been forced to content himself to control of rural eastern Congo, albeit a control continually eroded by attacks from Tshombe's forces.

It was Soumaliot's force which Che Guevara and his Cuban troops were to join up with in April 1965.

The third rebellion was based in the north where a force led by Nicholas Olenga captured Stanleyville in August 1964, threatening reprisals against its large white population if government troops tried to recapture it. The US and British-backed Belgian paratroop attack which was launched against the provisional government forces of Christopher Gbenye (one-time Minister of the Interior under Patrice Lumumba) in November was the event Che had attacked in his UN speech.

While this three-pronged revolt had captured a large amounts of territory, intense rivalry between the factions – some based on political semantics and the long-term ambitions of the principals, others along traditional tribal rivalry lines – combined to make an uneasy alliance which Tshombe's mercenaries found it relatively easy to divide and defeat time and time again, notwithstanding the development that Algeria and Egypt had joined China in supplying the rebels with more and increasingly sophisticated arms.

ABOVE Ex-President of Katanga, Mr Tshombe arrives at London Airport – April 1964.

AFRICA

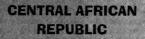

CENTRAL AFRICAN
REPUBLIC

SUDAN

Stanleyville
(Kisangani)

CONGO

KWILU PROVINCE

BELGIAN CONGO
(SUBSEQUENTLY ZAIRE, NOW THE DEMOCRATIC
REPUBLIC OF CONGO)

RWANDA

Brazzaville ★

KIVU PROVINCE

★ Bujumbura
BURUN

★ LÉOPOLDVILLE
(Kinshasa)

Fizi

● Kigoma
TANZAN

Luluaborg
(Kananga)

Albertville
(Katemie)

L. Tanganyika

KATANGA PROVINCE

ANGOLA

ZAMBIA

AFRICA

According to Froilán Escobar, Félix Guerra and Paco Ignacio Taibo II – authors of the first definitive account of Che's long-secret Congo campaign, first published in Havana in 1994, then in a French translation in 1995 which was masterfully summarized by Richard Gott in the London-based *New Left Review* early in 1997 – a volunteer force of 150 black Cubans had been recruited after the Belgian attack on Stanleyville, when Fidel Castro decided Cuba should provide positive help to the Congo rebels.

Based in three training camps under the supervision of Captain Víctor Dreke, a Cuban revolutionary war veteran who would later be a member of the Cuban military mission to aid revolutionary forces in Guinea-Bissau in the late 1960s, these troops (apparently selected on the basis that black soldiers would assimilate better with their African comrades) were told only that their eventual destination would be Africa, but not that it was the Congo.

They also did not know that the legendary Che was to be their leader. In fact, no-one in Havana was certain until he confirmed his decision to Fidel, on his return from Africa and China in March. It was only then that Dreke himself was informed that his volunteers would be going to the Congo, with Che at their head. The only other white man in the party was to be José María Martínez Tamayo (who would be known as 'Papi' in Bolivia), a senior intelligence officer whose most recent mission had been with a Cuban-backed guerrilla group in Argentina.

In the three weeks Che spent in Havana before leaving for the Congo, he reputedly underwent a drastic physical transformation, his disguise including a severe haircut (including his beard) and the removal of some teeth to change the shape of his now internationally-famous face. The first leg of his odyssey was a flight to Moscow, on board which was Luis Wanguemert, a Cuban TV journalist who had interviewed Che on many occasions. To Che's relief, Wanguemert did not recognize him.

From Moscow, Che and his small band (quite literally, as some were travelling with passports which said they were musicians!) flew to Cairo and then on to Dar es Salaam, the capital of Tanzania, arriving there on April 19 and awaiting the of arrival others who – along with the local revolutionaries – would make an eventual force some 410 strong. Among them would be the redoubtable 'Benigno' (real name Dariel Alarcon Ramirez), another Cuban War veteran who would also, later, accompany Che Guevara to Bolivia.

Before leaving Cuba, and perfectly aware that there was every chance that he may not return alive, Che got down to a little house-keeping as far as his personal and official lives were concerned. It was important that the Cuban government could distance itself from the Congo expedition if things went awry – a political device which does not reflect badly on Fidel Castro any more than it does on any government which disavows all knowledge of its intelligence operatives when they are captured. To this end, Che composed a 'farewell message' to Fidel which the Cuban leader would broadcast publicly six months later.

'I feel I have fulfilled that part of my duty which bound me to the Cuban Revolution on its own territory and bid farewell to you', Che wrote. 'Other nations are calling for the aid of my modest efforts. I can do what you are unable to do because of your responsibilities as Cuba's leader. In new fields of battle I will bear the faith you instilled in me, the revolutionary spirit of my people and the feeling that I am fulfilling the most sacred of duties . . . If my final hour comes under distant skies, my last thoughts will be for this people, and especially for you . . . '

More importantly, Che also renounced his Cuban citizenship, all his government posts, his rank of major in the Cuban army, and his various duties in the national leadership, so further distancing Fidel from any responsibility, if need be.

His Cuban family farewells were left with Aleida, in the form of a letter to his children (opposite page) which was to be opened only in the event of his death. He also wrote to his parents in Argentina.

The secrecy surrounding Che's presence in the Congo was so complete that not even the leaders of the National Liberation Council were advised of his impending arrival in Tanzania. It was a secrecy which would continue for close on thirty years; partly because of the Cuban government's embarrassment at Che's failure to achieve his objectives, and partly because not even Western intelligence services were able to get a clear fix on the his movements and activities during this 'lost' year, so making the few things they thought to be accurate both incorrect and therefore grossly misleading.

The immediate result of this secrecy was that there were no senior members of the NLC in Dar es Salaam with whom Che could discuss his plans. Gaston Soumaliot and Laurent Kabila were in Cairo on an extended stay during which they were attempting to settle their political differences with other Congolese revolutionaries. Instead, Che found himself dealing with Antoine Godefroi, a junior and under-empowered NLC official who nevertheless approved the Cubans' plan for a 14-strong detachment to make its way from Dar es Salaam to Lake Tanganyika. This they did on April 23, 1965, already aware that there was a huge gulf between them and the Congolese.

In common with many regional politicians, the NLC leadership rankled at outsiders trying to tell them how to run their revolution. Their agenda was local, not international, and was also confused by internal strife – hence the Cairo summit. If the NLC viewed their struggle as part

Dear Hildita, Aleidita, Camilo, Celia and Ernesto, If you read this letter one day, it will mean that I am no longer alive. You will hardly remember me, and the smallest among you will have entirely forgotten me.

Your father was a man who acted as he thought best and who has been absolutely faithful to his convictions.

Grow up into good revolutionaries. Study hard to master technique, which gives you mastery over nature. Remember that it is the Revolution which is important and that each of us, taken in isolation, is worth nothing.

Above all be sensitive, in the deepest areas of yourselves, to any injustice committed against whoever it may be anywhere in the world.

Yours always, my children. I hope to see you again.

A big strong kiss from
Daddy

of a wider scenario, it was a purely African one. According to Escobar, Guerra and Taibo, all of Che's attempts to broaden their vision were singularly unsuccessful.

Some NLC leaders also resisted Che's suggestion that Cuban training of guerrillas take place in the liberated eastern region of the Congo rather than in camps already established in China and the Soviet Union. This was largely due, Che suspected, to the extravagant life-style they enjoyed in exile, with unlimited access to wine and women a dominant factor in their thinking. Far better to train there than in the harsh reality of the Congo bush. From its inception, therefore, Che's expedition was working without the full support of the very people he had come to help.

A Swahili dictionary gave Che the codenames he and his colleagues were to use during the next eight months. Víctor Dreke became Moja ('One'), Martínez Tamayo became M'bili ('Two') and Che became Tatu ('Three') – an allocation of pseudonyms which confused the Congolese, who naturally assumed they also designated the seniority of the Cubans and could not understand why Tatu always seemed to give the orders.

After establishing a base at Kigoma, on the Tanzanian shore of Lake Tanganyika, Che and his party crossed to the Congolese village of Kibamba where they were greeted by a well-armed detachment of the People's Liberation Army. Language immediately became a problem (and one which would never go away), for while Swahili dictionaries helped them communicate in Tanzania, they were next to worthless in the Congo where a babble of tribal tongues were used. The only truly international language spoken (and then by precious few Congolese commanders) was French, and only Che was the only member of the Cuban force who spoke that.

The political in-fighting between the NLC 'partners' soon manifested itself in a complete lack of confidence in Antoine Godefroi on the part of the People's Liberation Army's (PLA) commanders. They rebuffed his suggestions that the Cubans be allowed to sit in on their planning sessions. Che revealed his true identity to Godefroi, thinking that it might help persuade the Congolese. Appalled at what he described as a potential *'scandale internationale'* and telling Che that 'no-one must know', Godefroi fled back to Tanzania to inform Laurent Kabila. His boss was, however, still embroiled in the Cairo talks and would not return to Dar es Salaam for some time.

Che's limited advance intelligence had not prepared him for the shock of encountering a small army of some 4,000 Tutsis from Rwanda. Fighting alongside the Congolese, they were refugees from a Hutu massacre which had taken place when Rwanda gained independence from Belgium and planned to return home once they'd helped achieve victory in the Congo. The military picture was far more of a jigsaw puzzle than Che had realized and he would never succeed in putting all the pieces together.

The PLA officers (still unaware of Che's true identity) did relent enough to invite him to present his plan. It was a classic orthodox guerrilla warfare scenario: a hundred men would be divided into groups of 20 for basic training in weapons and communications over a period of

ABOVE Joseph Mobutu – the man whose terrifying dictatorship Che could not overthrow.

MOBUTU

five or six weeks before being sent into action with 'M'bili' (Martínez Tamayo) at their head. At that time the most satisfactory soldiers could be identified – Che estimated that as being only one-fifth of the recruits – and re-grouped as a truly efficient force. The Congolese listened politely. Then they asked Che to submit it in writing.

While waiting for Laurent Kabila to return from Cairo, Che returned to his vocation as a doctor, working in a local dispensary. He was appalled to find a near-epedemic of venereal diseases among the PLA soldiers, all of them contracted in brothels on the Tanzanian side of Lake Tanganyika. In no way prudish, Che was not shocked by the prevelance of prostitutes, nor by the use of their services by the men; but he was by the thought that the men were paying for such services with funds intended for the revolution.

He was similarly distressed by the sight of what happened when new Soviet and Chinese supplies arrived at Kibamba. In the main, the Soviets sent medicines while Beijing despatched arms and ammunition. Unfortunately, most of the medical supplies were specifically designed for use in the field of battle, while the real need was for medicines which would be of benefit to the local population. And the chaos which attended the distribution of Chinese arms inevitably meant that men finished up with shells for the wrong guns, or weapons without key parts. When Che volunteered his Cubans as supply depot guards and distribution organizers, the PLA turned him down.

On May 8, more Cubans arrived at Kibamba. Led by Santiago Terry Rodríguez, a 35-year-old veteran of the Sierra Maestra campaign, they had travelled from Havana via Moscow, Prague, Paris, Nairobi and Dar es Salaam. While their arrival was a source of celebration for Che and his increasingly-impatient colleagues, an even greater cause of delight was the accompanying presence of Leonard Mitoudidi, a senior Congolese commander who combined fluent French with a fluid political brain. For the first time since he set foot in the Congo, Che was able to have a proper briefing of how things stood, both politically and militarily.

They were a mess, especially were they concerned the forces of Pierre Mulele, now bogged down in the centre of the Congo and inaccessible to outside aid. The Cairo conference had achieved little in long-term settlements between rivals, so a proper concerted front was still an idle dream. Mitoudidi, eager to help Che, arranged for the Cubans to be allowed to establish their base camp on Mount Luluabourg, some five kilometres and a four-hour march away. Cloaked in thick fog until late every morning, it was quite the opposite environment expected by the Cubans, who'd been told they would find themselves in – and had been trained for – a flat jungle terrain.

After refusing to countenance Mitoudidi's initial suggestion of a Cuban-led assault on the Tshombe stronghold of Albertville as far too ambitious at this stage, Che and Martínez Tamayo agreed, at a meeting with Mitoudidi and Godefroi, to carry out a four-pronged reconnaissance expedition.

While his colleagues investigated the country to the east, south and north, Che remained in Kilamba, his identity still a closely-guarded

ABOVE Che always kept his books with him – a quiet moment in the Congo.

secret, as was his person. Dreke and Martínez Tamayo's groups spent two weeks learning that while the area boasted a large number of 'friendly' troops, there was ample evidence that the enemy's positions were well-defended. Dreke, for his part, found Congolese morale low in the northern sector. He also caught sight of his first white mercenaries, near the town of Fizi, along with a a dusty landing strip just big enough for small planes and helicopters.

Che's own summary of the situation was characteristically succinct: the overall organization was incompetent and disorganized with the rebel rank and file having no respect for their officers who, in the main, 'spent days drinking, and then had huge meals without disguising what they were up to from the people around them'.

Organization and discipline could be improved, but the Cubans could not achieve that so long as they lacked interpreters. It was a frustrated Che who, at the end of May, was informed that 'a Cuban minister' was waiting to meet him on the Tanzanian side of the lake. It was Osmany Cienfuegos, who was one of the Cuban Revolution's senior leaders, visiting Dar es Salaam for official talks, who had taken the opportunity to visit his Cuban friends.

It was through Cienfuegos, who brought a new group of 34 more Cubans with him, that Che learned that his mother, Celia, was dying in Argentina. Despite his grief, he was able to update Cienfuegos on the situation during the next few days, with both men apparently agreeing that they had faced far less promising scenarios during their guerrilla days in the Sierra Maestra.

Before Che finally heard from Laurent Kabila, now finally back from Cairo but stuck in Dar es Salaam awaiting the arrival of Chinese leader Chou En-lai, the Cuban cause suffered a major set-back when Laurent Mitoudidi – their principal Congolese help-mate, friend and adviser – drowned in Lake Tanganyika. When they did hear from Kabila it was in the form of a letter delivered by 'Mundandi', the Chinese-trained leader of the Rwandan Tutsis. It only confirmed Che's conviction that the Congolese were being led by men who made major and over-ambitious decisions from positions far removed from the action they were, in theory at least, supposedly ordering.

In essence, Kabila instructed them to ignore Albertville but launch an attack on Force Benera, a government garrison inland from Kibamba, on the Kimbi River. Also the site of a hydro-electric plant, Benera boasted 300 of Tshombe's forces and some 100 Belgian mercenaries. The attack, Kabila ordained from the comfort of his Dar es Salaam HQ villa, was to be led by 'Mundandi', with 50 Cubans in support. And it should take place in a week's time.

Astonished and angry, Che tried in vain to renegotiate the terms of engagement. Many of his men were ill with malaria and in no condition to fight. It was more sensible to attack a smaller target so that the two forces could get to know each other better in action, especially given the fact that the Tutsis did not speak Swahili and only Che spoke French. Perhaps prisoners could be taken, to improve strategic intelligence on the enemy's situation and intentions.

ABOVE Fishing boats in the Congo, 1959.

Over-ruled by the locals, on June 20 Che watched as 40 of his men set off towards Bendera with 100 Congolese and Tutsi soldiers. If he was experiencing a sensation of impending doom, he had every right. The Bendera attack was, as he suspected, a fiasco.

Put simply, when the time came to attack, 60 men out of the 160 who'd left Kilamba had already deserted, many of the remainder had never fired a shot in anger, the Congolese members of the troop refused to fight and four Cubans were killed. Che was furious, even more because his own losses would probably lead to the enemy being able to confirm that Cuba was definitely involved in the Congo conflict.

So it proved. Documents found on one of the bodies – a diary and passport – told mercenary leader Mike Hoare that this particular casualty had travelled from Havana via Prague and Beijing, and had trained in both Czechoslovakia and China. Hoare had been tipped off (probably by the CIA, but maybe by deserters or informers) that Cuban troops had arrived, but the dead guerrilla's documents were a valuable bonus.

Che began to grow increasingly concerned. The Cubans' morale slumped after Bendera – if the people they'd come to help wouldn't fight, why the hell should they put their lives on the line? Even the arrival of 39 fresh reinforcements from Havana (some via Cairo and Nairobi, others via Prague and Algiers) only helped raise spirits a little, although Che's own were immeasurably raised by the sight of 'Pombo', the nickname of Harry Villegas, an old and trusted friend whom Fidel Castro had picked to become Che's personal bodyguard.

The group who'd travelled through Algeria brought grim news for their commandante. On June 19, Mohammed Ben Bella – Che's closest African ally and personal friend, founder of the Algerian National Liberation Front (FLN) and Algeria's first president after independence from France in 1963 – had been overthrown in a *coup d'état* led by General Houari Boumedienne. Che's isolation increased as international support for the Congo revolution began to flag.

Worse, an air attack on the new arrivals as they made their way across Lake Tanganyika indicated that Tshombe's forces were stepping up their organization. No Cubans had been lost in the incident, but it was a warning that things were likely to heat up in the near future. The belated appearance of Laurent Kabila in July – three months after Che and his first party had arrived to help fight his war – did little to create optimism. Kabila came with an entourage which included a number of women. It was more like a picnic outing than a war council, even more so as Kabila confided to Che that he had fallen out with Gaston Soumaliot, the other principal commander on the eastern front.

At the beginning of August the political waters muddied even further with news that Soumaliot had ousted Christopher Gbenye as head of the Congolese National Liberation Council, although he did not enjoy the same level of confidence or respect as Kabila.

With his own forces doing what they did best – harrying Congo government troops and Mike Hoare's mercenaries in a series of small, but largely successful engagements – Che wrote a remarkably frank message to his field soldiers in early August:

'We cannot pretend that the situation looks good. The leaders of the movement spend the great part of their time outside the country . . . Organizational work is almost non-existent since the middle-rank cadres do not work, do not know how to work and inspire no confidence in anyone . . .

'Indiscipline and the lack of any spirit of sacrifice are the principal characteristics of all these fighters. To win a war with such troops is out of the question' Che concluded. He also made it be known that he did not advise other African liberation movements to send their members to the Congo for training – the muddle and mess would destroy their morale too.

All Che could do was to try to reduce the inefficiency which surrounded him, initiating a training process very much like the one which the PLA commanders had rejected back in April. Discipline improved to a degree and there was no doubt that the Congolese benefitted greatly from accompanying the Cubans on their tightly-organized forays. Although Che was more circumspect in his reports back to Havana than he was in either his diaries or the missives he sent his field commanders, he does not appear to have been honest enough to ask Castro to order a Cuban pull-out.

In fact, Fidel's determination to increase Cuba's involvement in the Congo was as resolute as ever and in early September Che's forces were swelled by the arrival of a fifth group of fighters which included two serious heavyweights – Emilio Aragonés (who'd become known as 'Tembo the Elephant'!) and Oscar Fernández Mell, a Cuban Revolution veteran who would later become the Cuban ambassador in London.

Fernández Mell was also, perhaps just as importantly, a doctor. Che could always use another doctor because malaria had reached almost epidemic proportions in the Cuban ranks. He had suffered malaria himself, his discomfort aggravated by repeated asthma attacks.

But it was the presence of Emilio Aragonés which confirmed Fidel's commitment to the Congo operation. He was the organization secretary of his country's new governing party, the United Revolutionary Socialists. At first, Che feared that Aragonés had come with an order for him to return to Havana, but soon learned that both men had volunteered to serve in what they believed was a glorious and successful campaign. Fidel himself thought that Che's watered-down and diplomatically-phrased reports were too pessimistic!

Any hopes Che may have had for an honorable retreat from what everyone in his force knew to be a hopeless and probably unwinnable cause were dashed at about the same time when Gaston Soumaliot arrived in Cuba and gave Castro a glowing report of 'his' revolution's progress. Che had been unable to warn Fidel that Soumaliot was not to be trusted, but despite a message from Pablo Rivalta, Cuba's ambassador in Tanzania, warning Havana that Soumaliot should not be received and should not be promised any further aid, the Congolese leader was given the full red-carpet and brass-band treatment during his two-week stay and was told that 50 doctors would be sent to the Congo.

It may be that Rivalta's note was not given to Fidel Castro until that promise had been given, but before putting it into action Fidel decided to include José Ramón Machado Ventura, his Minister of Health, in a sixth group of guerrillas which arrived at Kibamba early in October. He immediately agreed with Che that it would be an error to send the doctors at that stage.

Casting off his gloves, Che wrote a bare-knuckle letter to Fidel explaining the situation: the lies that were fed to Castro by Soumaliot, the divisions between Kabila and Soumaliot, and the chaos and lack of organized revolutionary activity. He concluded:

'On our own we cannot liberate a country that has no desire to fight . .'

Even as he wrote those words, the truth of Che's last comment was confirmed by the steady advance of Moise Tshombe's mercenaries into the Cuban zone and Mike Hoare's ability to over-run Congolese rebel positions with ease. He was undoubtedly aided by the fact that he had far superior equipment at his disposal – the mercenary force which landed on the Congo coast of Lake Tanganyika in late September boasted six PT boats and an 80-foot gunboat, with air strike capability in the form of 12 Cuban exile-piloted T-28s, four B-26s and a Bell helicopter.

Hoare's first move was an attack on the rebel-held town of Baraka with two separate units of 100 men. A third 100-man team began an advance from Albertville towards Lulimba and Bendera. If Congolese and Rwandan positions posed little problem to his South African and Rhodesian troops, Hoare found the Cuban-trained rebels 'very different from anything we had ever met before'.

In his Congo memoirs Mike Hoare spelled out the difference: 'They wore equipment, employed normal field tactics, and answered to whistle signals. They were obviously being led by trained officers. We intercepted wireless messages in Spanish. One of my signallers was a Spaniard and said the language used was a very poor class Spanish, and it seemed clear that the defence of Baraka was being organized by Cubans.'

Eventually, inevitably, Baraka fell to the mercenaries and by the end of October Mike Hoare had also taken Fizi and was poised to head south towards Lulimba and Lubondja. Che pulled his forces back to their mountain-top base at Luluaborg and prepared for a long seige. It never came because politics intervened.

Moise Tshombe's use of white mercenaries had so outraged some other members of the Organization of African Unity (OAU) that, on October 13, the Congo's President Joseph Kasavubu was persuaded to fire his premier. Ten days later he told an African heads of state conference in Accra that, as the rebellion in the Congo was virtually over, he would order the mercenaries to leave. This gesture was enough for those members of the OAU who'd supported Gaston Soumaliot to withdraw their backing.

As these developments unfolded, Mike Hoare contacted the Congolese army chief, General Mobutu, for assurance that the mercenaries' contracts would be honored. Furious that he had not been consulted by Kasavubu, Mobutu persuaded the new prime minister, Evariste Kimba, to announce that the mercenaries would stay until the Congo rebellion was completely over. Indeed, many mercenaries would remain in the Congo until 1966, although Mike Hoare returned to South Africa in November.

On November 1 Che was advised by ambassador Rivalta that the Tanzanian government had decided to withdraw its aid and support from the Cuban force in view of the OAU decision. Shortly after, Fidel sent a message which, while noting Che's earlier remarks about the true Congo situation, left it open for Tatu (Che) to decide whether to stay or pull out. 'Whatever his decision, we shall support him', Fidel wrote, while adding pointedly: 'It is important to avoid annihilation.'

Che tried to persuade Fidel to get the Tanzanians to change their mind. Cuba did not back out of its commitments and this commitment had been made with Tanzania's full approval, with no time limits stated or imposed. Cuba should only abandon the Congo if the Congolese rebels themselves asked them to – 'but we should endeavour to ensure that this never happens.'

Aware that his Congolese 'allies' may well give up the fight, Che had an alternative plan ready: while the bulk of the Cuban force would leave, he and a hand-picked force of 20 men would stay to fight until all possibilities were exhausted. At that stage they too would pull out. There is also evidence that Che wrote to Chou En-lai and asked for Chinese help. Chou suggested that Che take no further part in combat, but

BELOW The Congo River.

stayed to recruit and train resistance groups. While this appealed to Che, Havana's response was a firm 'no'.

By all accounts, the last month had also witnessed a growing distance between Che and his beloved guerrillas, thanks to Fidel's release of Che's 'resignation' letter in October – a letter which now appeared to emphasize his renunciation of his position in the party leadership, his military rank and his Cuban citizenship. The gulf which opened reminded Che of the early days of the Sierra Maestra campaign when many viewed him as a stranger who merely 'happened to be in contact with the Cubans'. At a stroke, the bond he had done so much to create was torn asunder.

On November 20, the Cuban guerrillas – now a force of about 100 men – boarded three boats and departed from the Congo, watched by the enemy and hundreds of Congolese rebels. A few days later, most of the force took their seats on Russian planes bound for Havana, via Moscow. Che remained in Dar es Salaam to begin work on his campaign memoirs, in which he wrote of his last days in the Congo:

'I felt entirely alone, in a way that I had never experienced before, neither in Cuba nor anywhere else, throughout my long pilgrimage across the world.'

ABOVE Che with his children just before he left for the
Congo. From left, Aleidita, Ernesto Jr and Celia.

A Strange Farewell

Although Cuba's withdrawal from the Congo had been forced by circumstances way beyond its control, Che apparently viewed it as a personal defeat. No matter that he had been trying to operate in the worst possible set of circumstances, with language problems only one of many factors which made communications – that most crucial of elements in any conflict – both confused and confusing. He had also been pitched into battle with allies whose combat skills were minimal, whose dedication was dubious, whose conduct towards captives was often barbaric, and whose loyalties and agendas were fundamentally divided.

Within a week of Che's retreat to Dar es Salaam, General Joseph-Désiré Mobutu would overthrow President Kasavubu, declare himself head of what would become a one-party state and begin the systematic plunder of what was, potentially, one of Africa's richest nations. In 1971 his country would be re-named the Republic of Zaire, at which time all towns and regions lost their colonial taint and reverted to traditional African names. So, too, did Mobutu himself, adopting Sese Seko as the abbreviated version of a much longer and preposterous title/name (Sese Seko Koko Ngbendu Wa Za Banga) which, inter alia, ascribed to him the attributes of a fearless warrior adored by his grateful people.

Many of the rebel groups (still riven by rivalry) re-located to the relative safety of Angola, from where they would continue to inflict irritating flea-bite attacks on Mobutu's increasingly corrupt and brutal régime. While Mobutu would occasionally call on the French for support in quelling rebellions – including those of white mercenaries who pragmatically turned to Zairian exiles as their paymasters – both the Angolan MPLA and guerrillas led by Amilcar Cabral in Guineau-Bisseau were to benefit from the intervention and support of Cuban Army regulars during the next decade.

Far from being disillusioned by the Congo débâcle, Fidel Castro would elect to pitch a vast number of Cuban troops into a number of African ventures during the coming decade, including the war between Somalia and Ethiopia in the late 70s. According to the CIA, during the period 1977-1980, an estimated 27,000 Cubans were either fighting or working in no less than 16 African countries.

For his part, Che reportedly suffered a severe bout of understandable depression as he recovered his physical strength in the Cuban embassy in Dar es Salaam. He was joined there by his wife, Aleida March, and also by a Ministry of the Interior expert who would refine his disguise. According to his bodyguard, 'Pombo', Che left Dar es Salaam early in 1966 for 'a European country' (probably Czechoslovakia) where he spent 'several months' recuperating. Aleida stayed on in Tanzania before heading back to Havana to await her husband's return.

However, Pombo's version is contradicted by another account – that of his eldest daughter, Hildita - who says Che sent her a note, date-lined 'somewhere in South America', on February 1, 1967 – her 10th birthday. Other reliable sources place Che in Argentina during the spring-summer of 1967. It seems Che can definitely be placed in Havana in May 1966, but only in deep disguise and amidst the tightest security that not even his young family would be allowed a chance to breach.

Che had long been involved in planning Cuba's various South American ventures – most notably in Peru and Argentina in 1963-64. Both had ended disastrously, the Peruvian rebels led by Hugo Blanco being annihilated at the Peru-Bolivia border town of Puerto Maldonado in May 1963, while the Cuban-backed revolt of Argentine journalist Jorge Masetti was over-run and ended early in 1964, only months after his guerrillas crossed into north-west Argentina from a base in Bolivia.

(The third Argentine who helped initiate that doomed second campaign was Ricardo Rojo, a young lawyer Che first met in 1953, at the La Paz cocktail party, near the start of his second trans-continental trek).

Despite those disasters, Che had remained committed to Castro's ambition to translocate the victories of the Sierra Maestra into the cordillera of the Andes. Bolivia's jungle provided both an ideal training site and launching pad for guerrilla campaigns on the despised régimes of the neighboring states of Paraguay, Chile, Argentina, Peru and Brazil.

With this in mind, in March 1964 Che selected an East German woman, Tamara Bunke, to receive training in undercover intelligence work. Bunke, who would take the alias 'Tania', was an Argentine-raised Marxist who'd been recruited a year earlier by the Cuban secret service, and it was she who would set up her operation in La Paz, the Bolivian administrative capital, in November 1964.

Shortly after Che's return to Havana, the plan which would cost him his life 18 months later began to be put in motion. The first to go to La Paz, where he would be briefed by Tania, was the tireless José Maria Martínez Tamayo. Having shed his Congo alias, M'bili, he was to be henceforth known as 'Papi'. He would be called that when he died in the Bolivian jungle in July 1967. Tania herself was killed by Bolivian troops on September 6, 1967, her funeral made a public relations event by President René Barrientos, the man whose régime she was opposing

While plans were laid and communication made with the Bolivian Communist Party (their assistance, support and cooperation would be absolutely essential to the campaign), Che decided that he had to see his children one more time before he set off for the Bolivian jungle. A letter, to be opened in the case of his death, was not sufficient for him on this occasion and Aleida March was asked to bring them to his safe-house.

Still in deep disguise, and his real identity being thought too sensitive even for the children to know, the scene was set for what was – by any standard – a bizarre final family reunion which his daughter, Aleidita, would recall in 1987 for the Italian newspaper, *Il Tirreno*:

At the beginning of November, Aleidita's heavily disguised Daddy (whose passport said its bespectacled, pipe-smoking owner was a Uruguayan economist) and a small group of insurgents crossed the Argentine-Bolivian border and made their way towards their first rendezvous point, in the town of Cochabamba, some 80 kilometers south-east of La Paz.

Che Guevara's last great adventure had begun.

ABOVE Che relaxing with his daughter from his first marriage, Hilda Beatriz, February 1956.

RIGHT Hilda Guevara photographed in Havana, while her legendary father looks on – this time from a giant mural.

'The day came when she [my mother] took all of us to the house where he was. There we met a strange-looking man, bald, wearing glasses. He said he was Spanish and that his name was Ramón, and he said he was a very close friend of our father's. My father always sat at the head of the table . . . when the "Spaniard" sat there I rushed over to tell him that it was my father's seat, and that when he wasn't home I sat there . . . My mother told me later how proud he'd been that his five-year-old daughter should have reacted like that.

'Then he poured himself a glass of red wine. My father used to mix it with mineral water . . . I asked him: "How come, if you're such a good friend of my father's, you don't know how he drinks his wine? Here, let me show you." And I mixed his wine with water, which delighted him even more.

'A little later on he gave us some sweets, a box for each of the girls and one between the boys.

'When my father died, my mother showed me a photo of "Ramón the Spaniard", whom I remembered well. I remembered him taking my mother by the hand and talking to her with his head against hers. I said: "Mummy, what were you doing with that man who wasn't my Daddy?" She replied: "But he was your Daddy . . . " '

Back to Bolivia

The country into which Che and his guerrillas travelled in late 1966 boasts a history every bit as turbulent as any in South America. Part of the federation of states created by the Venezuelan-born 'Liberator', Simón Bolívar, in the 1820s (and named in his honor), Bolivia was previously the Spanish-ruled state of Upper Peru and had its own Pacific Ocean coastline until 1884 when the most serious of a series of territorial wars with various neighbors saw Chile seizing the coastal region, so making Bolivia the land-locked republic it remains to this day.

Although a 1904 treaty with Chile gave Bolivia unhindered rail access to the port of Arica, the Bolivians opted – in the main – to concentrate their principal export trade routes eastwards, via the Paraná river to the South Atlantic. This inevitably led to disputes with Paraguay (through which the river ran) which climaxed in the bloody 1932-35 war over ownership of the disputed Chaco border region in which an estimated 100,000 men died and Bolivia was overwhelmingly defeated.

Damaged national pride led to an army-led dictatorship coming to power in 1936. While notionally socialist, its suppression of true democracy was fascistic in its severity – most notably in the case of the 1942 Catavi tin-miners' strike in which many hundreds are known to have been killed when the military was ordered in to bring it to an end. Outrage at this led many leading opposition groups to unite as the National Revolutionary Movement (MNR) headed by Dr Victor Paz Estenssoro, an admirer of Argentina's Juan Perón. Also able to establish itself as an important faction in the national congress was the Marxist – and mostly pro-Soviet – Party of the Revolutionary Left (PIR).

In December 1943 the MNR supported a successful coup which brought Colonel Gualberto Villaroel to power, with Paz Estenssoro as his chief minister. This régime achieved little, save for the political mobilization of the indian peasants by the MNR and was consistently condemned as fascistic by its left and right-wing opponents. In 1946 the self-promoted General Villaroel was hauled from the presidential palace and hanged by a baying mob of PIR revolutionaries.

The succeeding PIR administration tried, but failed, to rule Bolivia for four years in an uneasy coalition with a number of old establishment parties. In 1950 it was dissolved and replaced by the more radical Bolivian Communist Party. Conservative power-brokers conspired to keep the MNR (which had meanwhile formed a new alliance with a small Trotskyist party with strong mining union links, so bringing labor activist Juan Lechín into their camp) out of office, even when the MNR was widely accepted as being victorious in 1951 national elections.

The Bolivian military intervened to create a junta government but, after a number of unsuccessful but increasingly violent revolts, the MNR finally overthrew the military régime in April 1952, by which time many workers and peasants had been armed and the army was almost completely destroyed. Installed as president, Paz Estenssoro rewarded his socialist supporters by nationalizing Bolivia's tin mines, breaking up the

BELOW The South American Liberator, Simon Bolivar

biggest privately-owned estates and granting indians land possession rights for the first time in history. However, as Che Guevara himself had discovered around that time, official treatment of native Bolivians still reeked of paternalism and a disdain which verged on overt racism.

It was not that which brought Paz Estenssoro down in 1956 but the runaway inflation his government was unable to control and which disenchanted his erstwhile supporters from Bolivia's middle classes. He was succeeded by the more conservative Hernando Siles Zuazo and inflation was halted, thanks to massive economic support from the United States which insisted that the most radical of Paz Estenssoro's social and political reforms be repealed or substantially curtailed. Obligingly, Siles Zuazo summarily ended the worker co-administration of the nationalized mine companies, and cut back various recently-expanded social services. He also invited American petroleum companies back into Bolivia for the first time since 1937, when Standard Oil of Bolivia had been confiscated.

Rather than signalling a return to liberalization, the political come-back of Paz Estenssoro in 1960 witnessed a consolidation of every policy introduced by Siles Zuazo, and the army's power being revived with US support. Paz Estenssoro's attempt to renew his presidential term for another four years in 1964 led to the MNR breaking up into rival factions, so allowing the military – again with US approval and CIA support – to overthrow his government.

Supported by many conservative elements and Bolivia's peasant masses, Paz Estenssoro's vice president, General René Barrientos, seized the presidency and proceeded to marginalize or outlaw most of the organized labour opposition. His arrival marked the beginning of a long period of military dictatorship and the process of conservative economic reform and political retrenchment. He also, shrewdly, tried to demobilize all popular groups, except the peasants who had achieved some degree of power as a result of the 1952 revolution. That power was greatly diminished, however, when Barrientos decreed that many of Bolivia's former major land-owners could reclaim their old estates.

A hot-bed of intrigue complicated by the fractiousness of the many rival political factions, Bolivia was a prime candidate for revolution, not least because the vast majority of its five million citizens (some two-thirds of whom were either mixed-race mestizos or boasted pure Quechua or Aymara indian ancestry) lived in abject poverty. The country's miners worked in appalling, almost medieval conditions and had no political rights whatsoever. Political debate was almost completely absent, as were the civil rights of those who crossed – or were suspected to have crossed – the military commanders, who effectively ran the government from top to bottom, and from the capital La Paz to every army outpost in the smallest provincial town.

But, as Che was to learn to his ultimate cost, there is a world of difference between a country being a prime candidate for revolution and its people being prepared to support such a revolution, especially when it was being fostered by outsiders. After three decades of domestic turmoil, broken promises, shattered dreams and a military régime whose severity

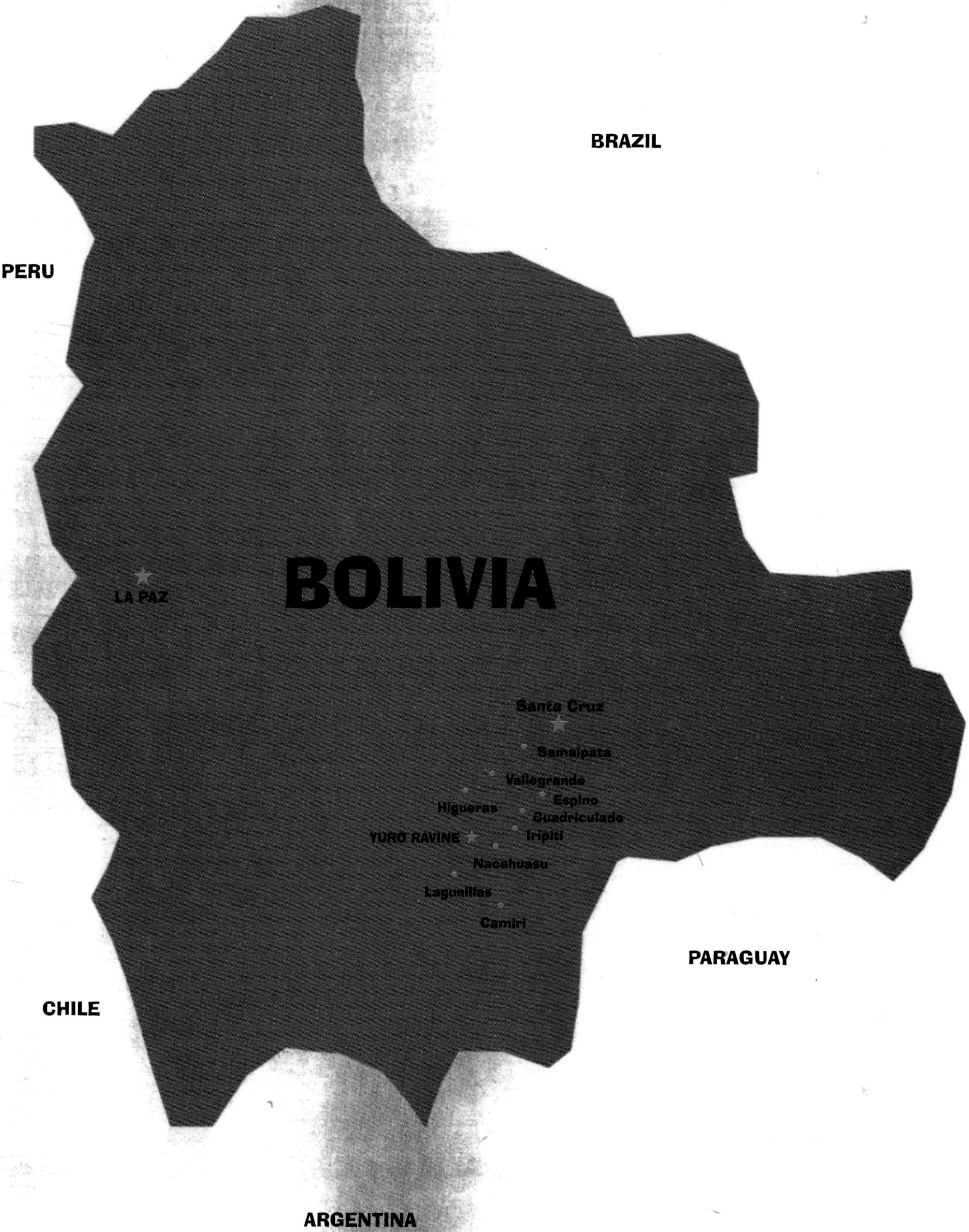

BRAZIL

PERU

BOLIVIA

LA PAZ

Santa Cruz

Samaipata

Vallegrande

Espino

Higueras

Cuadriculado

YURO RAVINE

Iripiti

Nacahuasu

Lagunillas

Camiri

PARAGUAY

CHILE

ARGENTINA

ABOVE General Rene Barrientos of Bolivia seen here with his wife, on a visit to Switzerland.

in punishment was terrifying, the great majority preferred to keep their heads down and their eyes fixed no further than the next row of maize plants in the fields they tended.

Che must have been aware of this, and must have known it was a world away from his only substantial revolutionary experience – the wilds of the Cuban hinterland where Castro's army had the immeasurable advantage of a populace eager for change. Recruitment was never a problem and if the finer points of Marxist theology went over their heads, their support for Castro was based on the undeniable fact that things could be no worse with him in charge.

If his Congo expedition had taught Che anything, it was that the Bolivian campaign was going to be a long haul, probably lasting years rather than months, with its eventual success or failure entirely conditional upon gaining the trust and covert support of the peasants, if not their political souls.

It was imperative that a local intelligence network be established as quickly as possible. To this end he needed to involve as many Bolivians as he could, with the local Communist Party's cooperation essential. Given Che's notoriously short fuse, he chafed at the long (to him) seven week delay between his arrival at the site of his first base camp – in the jungle near the Nacahuasu river and abutting the land of a farmer who thought the guerrillas were cocaine dealers! – and that of Mario Monje, Secretary of the Bolivian Communist Party.

Eventually brought to the rendezvous point by Tania, Monje arrived with three conditions for his support:

He would resign his leadership of the party, but would at least get its promise of neutrality. Additionally, he would recruit members to help in the forthcoming battles.

The political and military leadership of the struggle would go to him while the revolution was confined to Bolivia.

He would handle relations with the other South American communist parties, trying to enlist their support for the other liberation movements currently in train.

Che was stunned. In his contemporaneous notes he summarized his response to what consituted a bombshell: he said he disagreed with the 1st and 3rd points but would not object, however, he could not accept the 2nd point at all:

'We decided that he would think it over and talk to the Bolivian comrades . . . They all chose to stay and this seemed a blow to him'.

The simple fact was that Monje, in common with many Communist Party leaders around the world, found himself in the midst of a period of turmoil and schism which even then was dividing the movement. Increasingly the ideological edicts that emanated from Moscow did not match local requirements or realities on the ground. Splinter groups would depart to follow their own alternative readings of 'The Word'. Monje was also not alone in finding it impossible to persuade some of the members of his party to accept the intervention of outsiders in what they perceived as a purely internal, national, struggle that they alone should be fighting.

The only bonus in what Fidel Castro would later describe as Monje's treachery lay in the fact that the Bolivian members of Che's team had elected to stay with him. If they would side with 'foreigners', others would surely do the same. Monje's attitude also freed Che from any political compromise. If Monje left, in Che's own words, 'looking like a man heading for the gallows', on January 1, the new year dawned with the guerrillas' morale high and much achieved in the first two months.

Two primary camps had been established – tunnels and storage caves dug where arms, ammunition and other supplies (including Che's personal library of historical and political books) could be hidden, safe from prying eyes, to create the beginnings of what would eventually form a network of caches Che's men could draw on, or retreat to, if things got too hot for them in the coming months.

The Bolivians, although their commitment to Che had been fully confirmed by their rejection of Monje's ultimatum, were few in number and in severe need of military training. In that respect, Che had plenty of able help. By the time Tania brought Monje for the disastrous meeting, his fledgling force included at least three Cuban War veterans who could take them in hand:

Pombo (the alias of Harry Villegas, a native of Oriente Province who'd been Che's personal 'minder' in Columns 4 and 8 and was now a member of his Bolivian campaign general staff. Eventually rising to the rank of brigadier in the Cuban Army, Villegas would go on to undertake three tours of duty in Angola during the 1970s and '80s);

Joaquín (also called 'Vilo', in reality Juan Vitalio Acuña, a peasant from the Sierra Maestra who joined Castro's Revolutionary Army in April 1957 and was promoted to the rank of commander in November 1958. He had been elected to the Cuban Communist Party's central committee in 1965);

and Urbano (Leonardo Tamayo, another 1957 Sierra Maestra recruit, he had been a member of Che's Column 8 suicide squad and would go on to serve as a guerrilla in Nicaragua and Angola, retire from the Cuban Army as a colonel and take a post in the Ministry of the Interior).

In La Paz, meanwhile, Papi (José María Martínez Tamayo) was initially employed, with Tania, in coordinating the travel arrangements of further insurgents from Cuba, Peru and Argentina (the latter being former members of the ill-fated Masetti revolt who'd escaped capture), as well as the safe transit of weapons and other supplies. He would eventually join Che in the jungle to become a full combatant.

Among the other Cuban veterans who would also find their way to Bolivia were Marcos (the *nom de guerre* of Antonio Sánchez, a Column 2 veteran of the northern Las Villas campaign), Miguel (Manuel Hernández, a sugarcane cutter and magnesium miner who'd risen to the rank of captain in the Las Villas campaign), and Antonio (Orlando Pantoja, an early member of the July 26 Movement who had been imprisoned by Batistá, he'd joined the Revolutionary Army in October 1957 and had served as a captain under Che in Las Villas).

Last, but not least, was the formidable Benigno, in reality Daríel Alarcon Ramirez, who joined the Revolutionary Army at the age of 17

ABOVE Che (second from left) pictured at his Bolivian
guerrilla base in 1967.

and would, after the Bolivian campaign, become head of presidential security and the Cuban prison system as well as training guerrilla forces for duty in Angola in the 1970s. Ramirez retired in 1993, moved to Paris and enraged Castro with his book *The Life and Death of the Cuban Revolution*, which accused his former boss of creating 'a Stalinist régime'.

Much to Che's relief, the Bolivian contingent included a doctor, confusingly called either 'Moro', 'Morogoro' or 'the Doctor' in Che's notes (though his real name was Pareja), while a relatively early addition to the troop was a Bolivian medical student, ironically given the name 'Ernesto'. The real Ernesto, the former medical student whose rambles had led him along such strange roads away from his native Argentina, took the aliases 'Fernando' and 'Ramón' for this new venture, although his real identity was soon discovered and widely broadcast by the Bolivian state radio.

The doctor's skills were soon in great demand, not only to stitch and mend inevitable lesser injuries such as cuts and sprains, but also to tend the festering sores created by cattle-ticks which fixed themselves on exposed flesh and had to be ripped off with gruesome regularity. Even worse, perhaps, were the vicious little flies which burrowed under the flesh where they laid their larvae. These had to be cut out, a painful and bloody process. Che's asthma appears to have been quiescent during the early months – certainly, he made no reference to it in his diaries, which usually recorded attacks.

Heavy rain flooded the Nacahuasu river in mid-December, forcing them to abandon their first camp and move to Camp 2, but in the main Che filled his men's time by sending out a series of scouting missions to survey the surrounding country. The farmer who thought he was dealing with cocaine dealers became a useful source of provisions, but there were many times when supplies ran distressingly low.

From the very start, however, security proved a problem. The area in which they hid turned out to be popular with hunters. While they learned to keep low at weekends, Che was understandably concerned that his men inevitably left tracks as they moved about the jungle paths on their various forays. On one occasion, when Marcos and Benigno did not return from a scouting expedition, Che was able to follow their footprints for some distance before discovering that they had spent the night in the abandoned Camp 1! If he could trace their movements so easily, the same was surely true for anyone else – and they might mention what they'd seen when they returned home.

The Bolivians also had some problem grasping the concepts of tight discipline and seniority. Calling everyone together on December 12 Che had underlined the need for unity of command, announcing that Joaquín was his second-in-command, Alejandro had been appointed chief-of-operations, Pombo was chief-of-services, a man called el Nato was to be in charge of supplies and weapons, Moro in command of medical services, while Rolando and Inti Peredo were to be commissars, with Inti (one of the Bolivians) also given the finances to manage.

Their first brush with the authorities came on January 19, just as Miguel fell ill with a fever which Che suspected could be malaria. He wasn't feeling too good himself, but his symptoms did not worsen. Four guerrillas had arrived in camp with scavanged corn cobs but had also managed to lose a gun in the river. Worse was to follow when, at four o'clock that afternoon, the doctor arrived to report that a police lieutenant and four plain-clothes officers had arrived at Camp 1 in a jeep, apparently hunting for the cocaine factory the farmer, Argañaraz, had told them they would find.

They didn't, of course, but they did find a number of items which must have set alarm bells ringing in the provincial police HQ – carbide which fuelled the guerrillas' lamps and a pistol they confiscated from a Bolivian known variously as 'el Loro', 'Jorge' and 'Bigotes', who was supposed to be on sentinel duty. For some reason they did not take a Mauser and a .22 pistol which had also been left in the camp shack, but left warning el Loro that they 'knew everything' and he could have his pistol back if he came to the town of Camiri to claim it. The lieutenant, worryingly, asked for 'the Brazilian'– perhaps the farmer thought that was Che's nationality.

El Loro was, in fact, fast proving something of a liability. He had been driving the jeep which brought Che from Cochabamba to Nacahuasu and had almost driven off the road into a ravine when he learned Che's identity, forcing them to finish their journey on foot. On December 5 he'd caused a false alarm when he fired some shots without warning, and on December 26 he overturned his jeep, putting it out of commission for days. Between January 10 and 17 he simply wandered off, saying on his return that he'd gone to visit a woman friend!

Nevertheless, it was el Loro whom Che sent to threaten the farmer and a Vallegrande man who'd been hunting in the area, certain that one of them must have advised the police about their presence. Oddly, he also told el Loro to do as the lieutenant had suggested, and claim back his pistol at the Camiri police station. While there he was instructed to try to get in touch with Coco, the brother of commissar Inti Peredo, another Bolivian member of the team Che had sent to Santa Cruz, Bolivia's second-biggest city, on December 21, who had so far failed to return.

Oddly, apart from noting that he doubted that Coco was still at liberty, Che's diary does not include any sense of serious concern. At the very least, Coco's long absence was a potentially serious breach of security for, if he had been arrested, he could surely have been 'persuaded' to reveal Che's location to the authorities. If he nursed any suspicions that Coco had deserted the cause, Che didn't voice them, even to himself.

As it was, Coco re-appeared only two days later, as one of a party of four who'd been met by Pedro, at Camp 1, in the midst of a torrential rainstorm. He was bringing three new recruits – named by Che as Benjamín, Eusebio and Walter – to swell the guerrilla ranks. Benjamín was Cuban and knew how to use guns, which led Che to decide to place him in the advance party. The others were put in the rear.

To his discomfort, Che learned that Mario Monje had not only failed to resign his Communist Party post but had dissuaded three other newly-arrived Cubans from joining the guerrillas, and had written to Fidel Castro expressing his reservations with Che's objectives and repeating his

ABOVE Deep in thought, Che studies a map.

initial demands. Coco's mail-pouch contained one positive piece of news, however, in the form of a note from Tania in which she announced that she was departing for Buenos Aires, where she was to undertake a recruiting drive.

Recruitment and Che's morale would receive a boost on January 26 when Moisés Guevara arrived at Nacahuasu for talks. Accompanied by Loyola Guzmán, an attractive young Young Communist leader on the verge of expulsion from the Party for voicing her support of Che, Moisés Guevara (no relation to *el commandante*) was to prove every bit the opposite of Mario Monje. The communist leader of Bolivia's miners, he had split from Monje and was now offering Che his full support, including the much-needed replacement of the 70,000 pesos that Che had already spent.

Che spelled out his conditions for accepting the Bolivian's help. The existing structure of his group was to be dissolved. There would be no ranks for anybody until they had proved themselves. There was to be, for the immediate future, no political organization to the guerrilla group. There were to no polemics on the subject of national or international disagreements. Moisés Guevara nodded his agreement. His first manpower contributions would arrive some time between February 4 and 14, along with more powerful radio transmitters to improve communications between detachments.

In his month-end analysis, Che summarized Mario Monje's attitude as 'evasive at first and treacherous later.' Convinced that the Bolivian Communist Party was actually taking up arms against him, he was clearly encouraged by Moisés Guevara's response, though his optimism was guarded. **'We will see how he and his people behave in the future.'**

On February 1, 1967, Che Guevara and his force set out to find the enemy for the first time.

'Now begins the actual guerrilla phase and we will try out the group . . .Time will tell what the prospects of the Bolivian revolution are. The incorporation of Bolivian fighters has proved harder to accomplish than the rest of the programme.'

ABOVE A quiet day at the base camp.

Into the Dark

If the stereotype image of the guerrilla fighter is the one portrayed in big-budget Hollywood movies, rest assured that the first month Che and his insurgents spent out of their camp – patrolling the country in a wide arc from Camp 2 and hoping to test themselves in battle with the Bolivian army – was far more representative of the often grim reality of guerrilla warfare than the dynamic, thrill and incident packed exploits of the Stallones and Schwarzeneggers of this world.

Force marching their way through gulches, gulleys, swamps, marshland and swollen rivers (one of which would claim the life of the newly-arrived Benjamín on February 26, when he lost his footing and became the party's first fatality), they would encounter only a few isolated settlements and occasional family groups of peasants. But they found no soldiers, and no sign of soldiers, during the first 51 days they spent in the wilderness.

Hampered by the lack of accurate maps, this exercise nevertheless enabled Che to evaluate his force more completely. The truth was that he often did not like what he saw.

Physical fitness was lacking in many men, especially the Bolivians, although Che himself admitted (on February 23) to being 'completely exhausted and walking on will-power alone' after he'd come close to fainting as they topped a high hill. To add to their problems, many of the men's footwear was disintegrating rapidly as a combination of heat, cold and wet worked their damage on boots which were also battered by razor-sharp rocks and stones.

Che also began to note a visible break-down of morale and discipline, most alarmingly in the case of Marcos, one of those he should have been able to rely on unconditionally. Che had, in fact, encountered problems with Marcos from an early stage of the campaign. He had made what Che considered to be a few quite serious errors of judgement – errors which in fact had led Che to overlooking him when he announced the new command structure.

Marcos had been hurt by Che and Alejandro criticizing him in front of the Bolivians and by his lack of rank, especially given his experience. If Che thought Marcos had been pacified by the air-clearing conversation they had a few days later, he was mistaken.

Matters eventually came to a head on February 22 when Che 'overheard Marcos telling a comrade to fuck off, and during the day he said it to another man'. Che resolved to have words with him about this unacceptable behavior.

Three days later, Marcos missed the route the main party was taking and they lost all the morning in waiting for him. Che sent three men with a field radio – that Marcos had requested – but one (Pacho, a Cuban) returned a few hours later to report that Marcos was unable to pick up a decent signal.

Benigno was despatched to warn Marcos to return to base by six in the evening if he did not find the river he'd been sent to locate. With

BELOW The treacherous, tropical rainforests of Bolivia.

Benigno gone, Pacho reported that Marcos had given him 'arbitrary orders, threatening him with a machete and using its handle to hit him in the face'. When Pacho went back and told Marcos not to go on, he'd been threatened with the machete again, and even had his clothes torn when Marcos grabbed him violently.

A talk with Marcos and Pacho the next morning – after Inti and Rolando confirmed that Marcos' temper had already caused much ill-feeling in the advance party – convinced Che that while Marcos had not actually hit Pacho (who tended to exaggerate, if not lie outright), he was to blame for the original insult and threats of violence.

Criticizing Marcos for his attitude and warning Pacho that he faced a dishonorable discharge for both refusing to operate the radio and for not telling him about the incident earlier, Che called everyone together to warn them that he would not tolerate any such further incidents. Things were going to be tough enough once they engaged the enemy, without guerrillas fighting among themselves.

It was a few hours later that Benjamín slipped and fell into the rushing waters of the Grande, a river whose course they were following in a bid to find its confluence with the much bigger Rosita. Despite the best and bravest efforts of Rolando, Benjamín was swept away into a whirlpool. A tragic and tense day ended with Che's party eating the last remnants of their stock of kidney beans.

Things weren't looking good, and they got even worse on February 28 when it was decided to build a makeshift raft to cross the Rosita, which they had finally reached. During the crossing, Benigno's rucksack was swept overboard. More seriously, he also left his shoes behind on the far bank of the river.

Che's monthly diary summary was pretty mixed. Radio communication from the world outside had been regular, including coded messages passed on from Fidel Castro by Radio Havana.

One of these confirmed that Régis Debray, the French political writer who would be given the alias of Dantón, was on his way from Cuba via La Paz. There was, however, still no news from Tania regarding the possiblity of Argentine recruits. Other messages confirmed that the Bolivian Communist Party continued to be 'two-faced and hesitant', which did not surprise Che.

All things considered, Che thought the march had gone 'quite well', but he noted that 'the men are still weak and not all the Bolivians will last out. The past days of hunger have shown a weakening of enthusiasm which becomes more evident when we are divided.'

Of the Cubans he added:

'. . . two of the ones without much experience, Pacho and el Rubio, have not responded well yet, but Alejandro has done very well; of the old ones, Marcos gives me continuous headaches and Ricardo is not doing his best. The others are alright.'

March dawned with Joaquín reporting two of his men – Polo and Eusebio – of the theft of milk and sardines. This was serious. Rations were running dangerously low and theft of anything was, in any case, to be deplored. Che ordered that Polo and Eusebio should, 'for the time being', not be allowed to eat these foods when the others did.

Shortage of food was beginning to be a serious handicap, both to the guerrillas' progress and to their morale. A crop of tropical palm-tree hearts (known as *totai* in Bolivia) helped a little, as did the two little monkeys, a parrot and a dove which were caught on March 4, but everyone's physical condition was deteriorating badly. It was on that day Che's diary noted that his legs were beginning to show signs of oedema.

Living on scraps and the little they could shoot or catch in the forest, their spirits were raised on March 9 when a scouting party returned from an oil pumping station (the first sign of civilization they'd encountered) with a pig, bread, rice, sugar, coffee, some canned food and fermented corn. Che authorized a 'little feast of coffee and bread . . . and the opening of a tin of condensed milk . . . to make a sweet.'

But by March 16 matters had become serious once more. Che was admitting to serious fatigue and a number of men had swollen ankles, feet and legs. Protein was needed, and quickly. They eventually shot the party's pack-horse and had 'an orgy of horsemeat', although Che suspected that the next day would bring consequences. He was right, but not what he had in mind.

On their way to rendezvous with Joaquín, Miguel and Tomba attempted to cross the river by raft and had been swept away by the current, losing several rucksacks, six guns, almost all the bullets and one man, Carlos, one of the best Bolivians.

Three days later, with morale at a rock-bottom low, Che's advance party headed back towards base camp to find new arrivals in the shape of a Peruvian doctor, el Chino (just returned from Havana with more recruits), a radio operator, el Pelado, Tania, Moisés Guevara and the first

BELOW One of Che's Bolivian diaries – a gripping account of bravery, despair and eventual defeat.

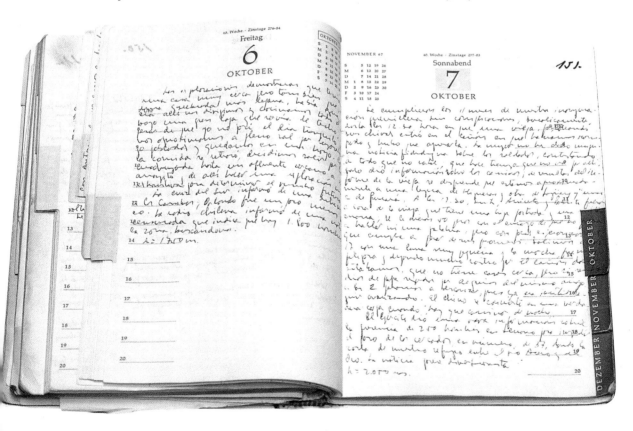

of his Bolivian volunteers – two of whom had already deserted – and Régis Debray, the Frenchman whom Fidel Castro himself had personally invited to join Che's Bolivian party.

Che was disconcerted to see a spotter plane circling above them, and to learn that it had been doing this for three days. Worse, Camp 1 – the farm base – had been attacked by a six-man police detachment and a 60-strong army force had captured a messenger from Moisés Guevara's group, along with a mule and a jeep.

Even worse still, Marcos had completely disobeyed Che's orders by being at the camp when the police attacked, and even though he and the others had evaded capture, Che was furious, ordering him to return from his hiding place.

As the various elements of Che's little army made their weary and dishevelled way into camp (three of Joaquín's men were barefoot), Che remarked on the 'climate of defeat' which pervaded the guerrillas. 'There is a terrible impression of total chaos', he wrote on March 20. 'They [his men] do not know what to do.'

Régis Debray thought the very same thing. Four years earlier he had spent time in the Venezuelan jungle, hiding out with guerrillas who had been encircled by the military, and were too weak and hungry to fight. But even then he had seen nothing like the dishevelled, rag-bag sight which met his eyes. His first impression was that Che Guevara was simply not in control of the situation.

Debray's presence in Bolivia was, in fact, due entirely to Che. While he was visiting Algiers, in January 1966, a mutual acquaintance had given the Cuban the current copy of *Les Temps Modernes* (a French political review published by the existentialist writer and intellectual Jean-Paul Sartre), which included an article by Debray entitled *Castrism, or Latin America's Long March*.

Che read it through and pocketed it. On his return to Havana he translated the article for Fidel Castro, who promptly invited Debray to be his pertsonal guest at the forthcoming Tricontinental Conference being held in Cuba.

While in Havana, Debray was asked if he would like to see the Bolivian campaign for himself. He could carry some messages from Castro to Che, stay a few weeks to gather material for a series of magazine and newspaper articles, and bring Castro any messages Che might have for him. Debray agreed readily and, despite his previous experience in Venezuela, underwent a brief and bizarre guerrilla training course, usually accompanied by Castro himself.

The contrast between that exercise and what he knew from personal experience to be the reality of life in the jungles of mainland South America, struck the Frenchman forcibly.

In his memoirs some years later – which were to outrage both Fidel Castro and the Guevara family when they were first published, and have remained a bone of bitter contention between the former allies ever since – Regis Debray pulled no punches in his description and analysis of this particular episode.

Fidel and his comrades dismissed the Venezuelan guerrilla actions he'd

ABOVE Che at work in the Bolivian tropical jungle.

witnessed as being 'bad planning badly executed', although Debray was convinced that they simply did not take into account that the Sierra Maestra was **'an Arcadia swept by cleansing winds in which there was no shortage of water, with no rattlesnakes or other poisonous vermin . . . reasonably populated, decorated with palm and banana trees, and easily accessible . . .'** while the mainland forests were, **'a slimy aquarium into which the light barely filters, a thick rubbery atmosphere through which the guerrilla fighter must tunnel his way with a machete, his bleeding feet wrapped in rags, his shoulders squared, thirty kilos on his back, on less than a thousand calories a day, his sleep fractured by sentinel duty, huddling in a damp hammock under a leaking canvas at night.'**

After only three months exposure to such inhospitable conditions, the Frenchman claimed that the distance between Che and his compadres seemed to be immense.

The 26-year-old Debray would be captured soon after leaving Che's brigade on April 19 and languish in a Bolivian prison for three years (facing 27 more under the terms of his sentence) until the French government negotiated his release and return to Paris. Later, in the 1980s, Debray would become President François Mitterand's principal adviser on Third World affairs.

Debray was to receive a rare insider's view of Che Guevara during his month in Bolivia and claimed that he was not impressed by what he saw, either of his disciplinary methods or his ability to communicate with his men. While he agrees with the still-loyal Benigno that Che was courageous and fearless, never asking others to go into action without him, Debray contends that Che's apparent inability – or wilful unwillingness – to explain his plans to his colleagues, was a flaw which was bound to prove fatal.

There certainly seems to have been no dispute over Che's decision to divide his small and still untested militia into three separate parties at the end of the month, with the 11-man advance party (including Benigno and el Loro) commanded by Miguel (Manuel Hernández), Joaquín's 13-strong rear party (including the unhappy Marcos and the doctor), and Che himself commanding the central group of 22 which included his long-time *aide de camp* Tuma, Moisés Guevara, Régis Debray, Alejandro, Rolando and Inti Peredo, Urbano (Leonardo Tamayo) and Tania.

Although Che was able to listen in to Radio Havana broadcasts on his short-wave radio, communications between the three groups on field radios were eventually to prove insurmountably problematical and he would – when the action began to hot up and they were separated by ranges of mountains and many miles of dense, often impenetrable jungle that not even the best machetes could slash through – be forced to rely on the propaganda emanating from Bolivian state radio in La Paz for the most meagre shreds of information about his brothers in arms.

By any definition, it was a haphazard and dangerous way to run a revolution. Very hit and miss, if you like. And while there would be the occasional hits, the misses were bound to lead, with an awful inevitability, to eventual failure and death.

The Long March

The six months during which Che's revolutionary forces were involved in direct action were absolutely typical of the early stages of all guerrilla wars. With a number of government troops known to be inexorably closing in on their positions, surprise ambush and rapid retreat was the insurgents' principal strategy.

These hit and run tactics, carried out successfully and over an extended period of time, have been proven by experience in innumerable conflicts, wreaking havoc on opponents' confidence and morale, and helping aid the recruitment of the 'host' country's disadvantaged and disgruntled poor in whose cause the revolutionary forces are fighting.

In Che's case, however, the Bolivian army's overwhelming superiority on the ground (and, more tellingly, in the air, thanks to spotter planes and helicopters) meant that he lost control of the situation at a fairly early stage. Few of the ten skirmishes in which his ever-dwindling band were involved between March 23 (when they ambushed an army patrol near Nacahuasu and enjoyed a rich haul of weapons, ammunition and intelligence information from voluble prisoners and captured documents) and the final fatal confrontation in Yuro Ravine on October 8, were strategically important or promoted his long-term objectives in any way.

An increasing amount of Che's time was spent in hiding, repeatedly forced back into the jungle which – as injuries and illnesses mounted – became as much a hell-hole as home or refuge. Reinforcements could not be found or brought into the war-zone and the locals did not rally to his cause, thanks in main to the brutal and punitive methods employed by army commanders when they suspected peasants of complicity.

The first Cuban fatality of Che's Bolivian war came on April 10 when an 11-man group of forward and rear party members combined to ambush 15 soldiers who'd been spotted heading downriver at Iripiti. During the first burst of gunfire Jesús Suárez Gayol ('el Rubio') was hit in the head by a bullet. Although six soldiers were captured, four managed to escape and raise the alarm. Later, when more troops arrived, they fell into precisely the same ambush, failing to take any precautions.

It was an impressively successful encounter, leaving ten soldiers dead (including two officers), six wounded and Che in charge of 30 prisoners, one of whom was a major. From these he was able to learn that they were part of the same 100-strong company who'd been hit by his force on March 23. Under the command of the 4th Division, their number included some paratroopers and a number of local soldiers who Che described as 'almost children'.

After burying Suárez Gayol in a makeshift shallow grave, Che released his prisoners (after stripping them of equipment and clothes), and sent them packing with a message for the authorities. To his discomfort, the evening radio news bulletins included a first-hand and detailed description of the first base camp by a Chilean journalist who'd been taken there, including the fact that he'd discovered a photograph of beardless, pipe-smoking Che. His disguise had been broken.

ABOVE A procession of Bolivian Soldiers, the modern
photograph shows their continuing presence.

With Joaquín ordered to go ahead and establish a presence in the area near the town of Muyupampa (his rear party had already come under fire from the air), Che's progresss towards the town he intended to capture was slowed by Tania and Alejandro, both of whom had fallen ill with fever, and Moisés Guevara, who was suffering a gall bladder infection.

Che also determined to let Régis Debray leave the party about this time, feeling that he would serve his cause better as a messenger between Bolivia, Havana and Manila, where a growing Communist Party support for his campaign was becoming manifest. Before that could happen, however, on April 19 they encountered an English civilian called Roth who initially claimed to be a journalist but eventually admitted to being a Spanish language teacher with the US Peace Corps in Buenos Aires.

To show good faith, Roth offered to help Debray and Carlos (a Bolivian who was headed for Argentina on a recruiting drive) to get out of the area. As Che delivered a surrender-or-die ultimatum to the authorities in Muyupampa, he also gave Debray a number of coded letters for Fidel and others – and a shopping list of books he wanted the Frenchman to bring him when he returned! As Gibbon's 18th century classic *The Decline and Fall of the Roman Empire* headed the list, Debray assumed that Che intended to remain in Bolivia for a long time.

The first news of Roth, Debray and Carlos came the next day in a radio news item which said they'd been captured and arrested for being in possession of forged papers. That evening the authorities gave their answer to Che's ultimatum by sending three fighter bombers in to attack the house in which he'd set up base. Only one of his men was injured by shrapnel, but it was a clear sign that Muyupampa was not about to surrender. A retreat was in order.

On April 22 Che's detachment captured a small truck and a number of horses in an action which he described as 'negative' and marked by bad discipline and bad planning. Although they'd increased their mobility, they lost a wad of dollars which Pombo had in his pocket and did not receive provisions for which they had paid some peasants. As Che noted in his diary: 'We still have a long way to go before we turn this into a combat force, although morale is quite high.'

Three days later that morale was hit near the village of Elhezon when Rolando San Luís – one of Che's best guerrillas and a friend since he'd been a Column 4 messenger in the Sierra Maestra – was killed as the revolutionaries tried to ambush a force of some 60 Bolivian soldiers. A bullet shattered both his femur and his nervous-vascular system, and although Che and the doctor tried to give him plasma, Rolando had lost too much blood before his body had been retrieved.

Meanwhile, in a separate but parallel incident, Benigno and a guerrilla named Aniceto had been surprised by an army ambush near Nacahuasu. Although they escaped unscathed both men had lost their rucksacks, and the very presence of the army troops – and helicopters – near Nacahuasu suggested a pincer movement was being conducted by the enemy, which meant that both of Che's initial route options were now closed. It was clearly time to make their way into the deepest part of the jungle and await news, if any, of or from Joaquín's party.

Che's monthly summary expressed concern at the loss of el Rubio and Rolando, the arrest of Debray and Carlos, official broadcasts which confirmed that US military 'advisers' (in the form of Green Beret paratroopers) and helicopters had been added to the Bolivian army's strength, and the fact that the last skirmish had resulted in no more than the death of two police dogs. He accepted that dividing his forces had reduced the guerrillas' effectiveness, but felt able to sum up April as **'a month in which everything has evolved normally, considering the development of a guerrilla war.'**

May dawned with a brief celebration of May Day by opening up trails, but their relatively slow progress would characterize much of the month – a slow, long and hard slog.

There would be occasional encounters with stray military detachments, but they served mostly to keep the dog-tired and often ailing revolutionaries on their guard at all times. The radio kept Che informed of Régis Debray's progress and the fact that General Barrientos intended to ask the Bolivian parliament to re-introduce the death penalty, and also told him that el Loro (who had vanished during the April 22 fiasco) had escaped from captivity in Camiri.

Food was not a major problem at this stage, as is evidenced by the pig roast (with rice, fritters and pumpkins to help make it a feast) they enjoyed during the evening of May 12, at a house they had previously visited and where the hospitality was generous. After days of short rations everyone ate too much too fast and Che noted that the result, on May 13 was a **'Day of belching, farting, vomiting and diarrhoea; a real organ concert. We stayed absolutely motionless, trying to digest the pig . . . I was very ill until I vomited and felt better . . .'**

By May 29 Che's force of 25 had struggled to reach the outskirts of Espino, a Guaraní indian settlement, but only after wandering into the townships of Caraguatarenda and Ipitacito in broad daylight and stealing merchandise from a shop in the last-named village. Following the rail track to Espino they lost a Ford truck they'd 'liberated' from employees of an oil company in Caraguatarenda – along with another truck and two jeeps – when its engine blew up.

The next day, intending to push on to the town of Muchiri, Che's sentinels sprang an ambush on an army patrol, killing three men and wounding one. Retiring from their positions at Cuadriculado, Che and his party began a 12 km walk towards where Miguel was supposed to be waiting with one of the jeeps. It had broken down, its radiator bone dry. One by one the men lined up to urinate into the reservoir, so enabling them to drive on for a rendezvous with the others!

The jeep was kept in service for the next few hours, but was eventually abandoned when it ran out of petrol. Shortly after, a group who'd been sent to find fresh water managed to ambush two army trucks, killing two men. That little success was marred by the loss of el Nato's anti-tank grenade launcher which exploded when he tried to fire it. Fortunately, the guerrilla escaped injury.

Che's diary entries for May ended with continued concern about lack of contact with Joaquín (who had, in fact, headed further north) and his

ABOVE A farmyard in the Bolivian highlands.

'total failure' to attract peasants to his cause ('it is a slow and patient task'). On the plus side, however, Che felt that the publicity surrounding the Debray case had given 'more combat power to our movement than ten victorious fights', and there were no signs that the Bolivian army was any better organized, nor that its technique was getting substantially better. Most importantly, three new battles (with losses to the army but none to the guerrillas) and penetration into Pirrenda and Caraguatarenda could be viewed as a military success.

Che celebrated his 39th birthday on June 14 without ceremony. Instead, he and most of his party spent most of the day freezing at a watering place, awaiting news from Miguel and Urbano who were attempting to force a path through to the Grande river. That evening they ate the last of their stew, leaving them only one ration of peanuts and three of stewed corn.

It was, in many respects, a typical day in a month which saw little real action with only smatterings of information gleaned from the radio. Two days before his birthday, for instance, the news broadcast included an announcement that three of Joaquín's guerrillas had been killed, only mentioning Inti (not the Peredo brother) by name but listing the numbers and various nationalities of Che's little army – 17 Cubans, 14 Brazilians, 4 Argentines and 3 Peruvians. It was uncomfortably close to being spot-on, so someone must have talked.

Someone who was saying more than Che felt comfortable with was Régis Debray. The subject of a number of interview features on the radio, Debray was talking up the revolution splendidly, but there were times when his bravado under questioning came dangerously close to being rather too specific in its detail.

(In later years, Debray would have to defend repeated allegations that his self-promoting machismo had somehow contributed to Che's capture and death, enabling the authorities to get a better fix on the guerrillas. This was patent nonsense, of course – Che's activities had been a matter of public record for some months before Debray arrived in Bolivia, while the guerrillas' locations were identifiable simply from reports of the various skirmishes and encounters they'd had with the military.)

On June 24 Che's spirits were raised by news of fighting between miners and troops at Bolivia's Siglo XX Mine. While that particular revolt would be quickly subdued by the massacre of almost 100 strikers, Che took it as proof that the presence of his force was beginning to energize the Bolivian populace. He needed cheering up – with his medicine supplies dangerously low, asthma had begun to be an equation in his own personal fight.

He would need all his emotional reserves on June 26 ('A black day for me', he opened his diary note) when the guerrillas' ambush positions on the banks of the Secco river were subjected to a surprise and well-planned retaliatory attack by army troops. In the melée, Pombo and Tuma were wounded – Pombo only superficially, in the leg, but Tuma fatally. Hit by a bullet which destroyed his liver and perforated his intenstines, he died as Che, his long-time friend and father-figure, tried desperately to save his life on a make-shift operating table.

Before he died, Tuma gave his wristwatch to another guerrilla, asking him to pass it to Che in the hope that his compadre would one day be able to give it to his family back in Cuba. It was something Che had done for others in the past. Solemnly, Che slipped Tuma's watch onto his own wrist and we can only assume it was still there on October 8 when Che himself fell in action.

Despite the continued lack of contact with Joaquín, Tuma's death and Pombo's leg wound making him a constant straggler, Che's monthly summary was remarkably optimistic. Morale stayed firm, as did the will to fight. His most urgent task was to re-establish contact with allies in La Paz, to re-stock medical and military supplies and recruit 'about 50 to 100 men . . . even if the number of combatants is never more than ten or fifteen people in action.'

That may have been ideal, but it was never realistic, and certainly not when the Bolivian army continued to move in, its intelligence boosted by information gained from informers and terrified peasants, most of whom resolutely refused to join the rebel cause. The truth was, Che's little army was increasingly going round and round in ever-decreasing circles and none of its actions were having an appreciable effect in real terms. With another month gone they had fought only two small skirmishes, lost a valued and valuable fighter and could only claim four enemy dead, with another merely wounded.

BELOW Floating logs in the Beni River, Bolivia.

July began with a push towards the town of Barchelón before following the course of the Piojera river through a canyon. Repeatedly circled by a spotter plane, they were also forced to stop for a day so Pombo's leg could be rested. On July 6, near the mountain-top settlement of Sumaipata, Che once again decide to carry out a day-time operation (in itself foolhardy – much better to operate under cover of darkness) to seize the local police station, buy some medicines at the pharmacy, foodstuffs from a store and raid the hospital for further much-needed medical supplies.

Learning that there were no police checkpoints at Sumaipata, Che ordered six men to stop and hijack a truck, drive it into town and carry out their smash-and-grab exercise. They stopped a truck coming from the direction of Santa Cruz but, a few moments later, were joined by another whose driver stopped to offer help and got into an argument with a woman passenger who refused to climb down from the cab. Within minutes two more trucks had pulled up and a full-scale gridlock traffic jam had been created.

Driving into town, the men over-ran the police station and military post in brief actions which resulted in the capture of a number of weapons. Although some vital medicines were brought back, they did not bring the drugs Che needed for his now rampant asthma. With the whole episode witnessed Sumaipata's small population and a group of travellers, Che knew that news of the exercise would spread like wildfire. It was time to move out, and as quickly as possible.

It's difficult to understand why Che would have exposed himself and his force to such a high-risk venture. One must question the judgement of a man who would order such an action when the same supplies – especially the drugs he so badly needed – could have been secured by a couple of men strolling casually into town when night fell and simply buying them from the pharmacy. In the meantime, the whole district was alerted to their presence, a soldier had died in the exchange of gunfire, and Che Guevara had given the authorities yet another excellent reason to step up their remorseless hunt for him.

For the next three weeks the guerrillas stumbled around the countryside, replenishing their provisions when they could and listening to the radio every night. On July 12 it told of a military action against guerrillas on the Iquiri river – undoubtedly Joaquín's party – and the death of one insurgent, whose body had been taken to Lagunillas. There was also news of a growing split in the government of General Barrientos, including the formation of a political party 'of Christian inspiration' by agricultural syndicates in Cochabamba which called for national unity in the face of Che's 'invasion'.

Che learned that his *Message to the Tricontinental: Create two, three . . . many Vietnams* leaflet had been published in a long coded message he recieved from Raúl Castro on July 24. Reaction had been mixed, with some critics describing the Cuban revolutionary as 'a new Bakunin' (a reference to the legendary Russian anarchist Mikhail Bakunin who opposed Karl Marx), and 'deploring the blood spilled and that will be spilled in the case of three or four Vietnams'.

Of greater concern to Che were reports of two military actions against guerrillas. As these were some way apart he couldn't be sure if this was mere government propaganda, but July 26 broadcasts (after which Che gave a talk on the significance of that date for the non-Cubans in his party) on foreign stations describing the one which had taken place near the town of San Juan del Potrero had all the trademarks of authenticity. So, Joaquín's party was still active, and were on the other side of the Cochabamba-Santa Cruz highway, some 50 km away.

On July 27, Che's band were involved in their second substantial brush with the army when an eight-man ambush detail hit the first four members of a similarly-sized group of soldiers making their way along the banks of the Seco river. Three soldiers were killed and a fourth wounded, but no weapons were seized as the other four soldiers had taken cover and could have opened fire on any guerrillas attempting to scavange supplies.

At dawn the next day, as Che's party were preparing to push on to the house of Paulino, a rebel sympathizer, they were attacked by a large force. In the first flurry of fire, Miguel managed to capture a rifle and cartridge belt from a wounded soldier, along with the disturbing information that a force of 21 soldiers was on its way to the nearby town of Abapó, while another 150 were already based in Moroco – all too close for comfort and a much more serious threat than had previously been posed by the military. Worse, all the male inhabitants of Moroco had been arrested and taken in for interrogation.

Hurrying up his men, Che and Pombo crossed the river canyon under fire, heading for a spot where the trail ended and they could set up defensive positions. Che sent Miguel, Coco and Julio ahead to form a forward position, leaving 12 men to cover the main party's retreat. He had just ordered a halt to rest in the first available good position when Camba came to report that Ricardo and Aniceto had fallen while crossing the river.

Ordering Urbano, el Nato and León to go on horseback and find Miguel and Julio, Che's group pushed on up the trail, only to be met by Camba with news that Miguel and Julio had been taken by surprise, but had retreated safely and were awaiting his orders. Che ordered him and Eustaquio back, leaving him with only Inti, Pombo and el Chino.

It would be three hours before he had a full picture of his losses – the guerrilla known as Raúl was dead (a bullet through his mouth), but Ricardo and Pacho had escaped with wounds. Ricardo's injuries turned out to be fatal however, and, as the last batch of plasma had been lost in the confusion, along with eleven rucksacks containing vital medical supplies, binoculars and the tape recorder used to copy coded radio messages from Havana and Manila, he died nine hours later, his burial place being a well-hidden spot on the riverbank where the government soldiers were unlikely to find it.

Pacho, on the other hand, would survive what must have nevertheless been an embarrassing wound. The bullet which passed through his buttocks also penetrated the skin of his testicles, making his future mobility a matter of severe discomfort.

Che's diary notes on the encounter were characteristically clinical concerning his lost comrades. While mourning Ricardo's death

'He was an excellent fighter and an old comrade in adventure . . . in the Congo and now here. His quality makes him another important loss', Che also described him as 'the most undisciplined of the Cuban group and the one who showed the least decision when facing up to everyday sacrifices'.

Chillingly, Che noted that Raúl's death **'hardly counts, considering his introspective nature'.** He wasn't, in Che's opinion, a good fighter or worker, although **'he was always interested in political problems, even if he never asked any questions'.** It was a callous dismissal of a man who had been prepared to die for his beliefs.

The month had not been a military success and there were signs that the Bolivian army was finally getting its act together. As it drew to a close, Che listed his most urgent tasks to be – re-establish contact with Joaquín and La Paz, recruit combatants to supplement his depleted and ever-weary 22-man group and get medicines. Apart from a growing catalogue of injuries and illnesses within the group, his asthma had returned with a vengeance.

By August 8 Che admitted to being 'a human wreck' as petty squabbles broke out among his party. Progress was excruciatingly slow as teams of men with machetes tried to hack a path towards one of the supply camps established in the first few months, aware all the time that they now faced the constant peril of attack from the dense undergrowth around them.

At a meeting Che called that evening, the majority voiced their determination to carry on regardless, but the arguments left him dispirited, as did the need to lance an abcess which had formed on his heel, making walking an agony. He also noted that mosquitoes were a continual plague wherever they set up camp.

Disaster struck on August 14 when the radio news told them that the camp towards which they were inching their way had been discovered. Che had asthma drugs stored there and they would have been taken – along with the documents and photographs the broadcast said had been captured. **'It's the hardest blow they could have inflicted on us'**, Che wrote that night. **'Somebody talked. Who? We don't know that'.**

A possible answer came the next day in news that two prisoners had been taken **'from the Muyupampa group, which is undoubtedly Joaquín's. Our men must be badly harassed and, to top it all, those two prisoners talked'.**

Matters deteriorated and the group was forced to kill one of their packhorses to add meat to their meagre rations, which at one time included the rotting corpse of a cat someone found while hunting for something more palatable. The doctor (Moro) began to flag badly, apparently with lumbago, and Che was forced to inject him with a local anaesthetic to keep him reasonably mobile. Even more alarming, although some members of an eight-man scouting party led by Benigno (which Che had sent out on August 9) returned from their various tasks, it was not until August 27 that he, el Nato and Julio re-appeared safely.

Before that, on August 26, an ambush Che had laid for a seven-man army company as they crossed a river went badly wrong. Two of the soldiers managed to run off when Antonio fired too early and the other five managed to find positions from which they could repel the rebels. In the chaos, Che realized that some of his men were in danger of being hit by cross-fire from other members who were located on the other side of the soldiers. Furious, he ordered the ambush to end before the escapees returned with reinforcements.

As Che's red-faced combatants retreated, an army force of some 30 men hove into view. Discretion was clearly the better part of valor and the retreat continued.

Benigno's team brought more dark news. The cave hideout which had been Che's next intended destination was now an army base in which some 150 soldiers were encamped. There were soldiers, too, at two safe-houses they'd intended to visit for information and supplies, while a third was now abandoned.

Battling on, with hunger and thirst driving morale down to an all-time low, another horse had to be sacrificed for sustenance and some men were forced to drink their own urine as they tried to hack a way through the jungle, with diarrhoae and cramps the inevitable result. The month ended with Che aware that his own diminishing strength was adding to the team's doubts. So far, only one – Camba – had actually expressed his by suggesting that he be allowed to leave, but Che was aware that others were beginning to feel the same.

With the military presence (aided by regular over-flights by spotter planes and helicopters) now posing a very real threat, September was always going to be a crucial month and its mere survival a real priority if Che's little army could hope to continue in its mission in the long-term. Conditions improved a little as they returned to the Nacahuasa river valley with its better supply of food and water, but the news did not.

By all accounts, Joaquín's force was being hit hard. On September 2, a news item on The Voice of America radio channel claimed that a group of 10 men 'led by a Cuban called Joaquín' had been killed in the area of Camiri. Che was unsure, especially as the local radio stations had said nothing in their news, and a further Voice of America broadcast which named José Carillo as the only survivor did nothing to persuade him that it was anything but propaganda. Although Carillo was one of Joaquín's band, the battle was reported to have taken place by the Masicuri river, which could not be correct.

The next day brought news of another death in Vado del Yeso, near where the party of 10 was reputedly killed. While this reinforced Che's belief that the Joaquín story was false, it contained accurate details of the Peruvian doctor and el Negro, whose bodies had been identified by the guerrilla el Pelado, who was already being held in Camiri.

On September 7, the Santa Cruz radio station announced that the body of the female guerrilla, Tania, had been found on the banks of the Grande river. Piling on the agony, it also said that José Carillo, the

survivor of the Joaquín massacre, had confirmed that Régis Debray had carried a gun and taken part in military duties while staying with Che, so blowing Debray's principal trial defense – that he was a mere jobbing journalist – out of the water. Che was furious with Carillo's treachery, vowing in his diary to 'make an example of him' when the war was won.

Confirmation of Tania's death came with news of her funeral on September 8, which was attended by a triumphant General Barrientos. Three days later, Barrientos displayed his fine grasp of logic by announcing, in morning broadcasts, that Che had been dead for some time and that all recent news had been mere propaganda. Later in the day he returned to the microphone to offer a 50,000 pesos (about $4,200) for information leading to Che's capture, dead or alive!

On September 15, the radio told Che that Loyola Guzmán, his pretty ex-Young Communist Party cohort, had been arrested. She would stage a number of hunger strikes and her arrest would also cause a national teachers' strike in sympathy, further news of which continued to find places in Che's diary. But these were eclipsed in importance on September 22, when General Barrientos held a press conference to confirm that all of Joaquín's force were either dead or captured.

Che really was on his own.

ABOVE More the pose of a politician than a guerrilla –
Che plays with two peasant children, only hours before
his capture.

Disaster and Death

On September 7, Che's diary notes included a strange question-and-answer exchange in which he asked himself of the enemy and the general situation:

'Are they afraid? Not likely. Or do they consider the way up to here impossible? With the experience of what we have done and what they know, I don't think so. Are they letting us advance, to wait for us at a strategic point? It's possible. Do they think we will have to go to the Masicuri area for our supplies? It's also possible.'

Despite his certainty that the Bolivian authorities would be preparing a major ambush for him somewhere along the way, and despite knowing from bitter experience that there were now huge numbers of soldiers in every decent-sized community in the area, on September 18 he ordered his men to begin what would be an eight-day march – much of it along public roads and in full view of frightened peasants, local government officials and potential bounty-hunters who would love to claim that 50,000 peso reward Barrientos had offered.

Che's objective was to reach Higueras, where he knew both food and now-vital medical supplies could be found. While one cannot disapprove of that objective, it was almost lunatic to attempt it with a forced march involving men who were already on their last ounces of physical and mental reserves. Petty arguments had begun to flare into furious disagreements, as frayed tempers snapped and Che's almost-legendary strict discipline had come into play with a vengeance.

The guerrilla Chapaco had been punished with six days' extra duty for disobeying an order; Benigno was lierally reduced to tears by a furious Che when he allowed himself to be spotted by some peasants; and Pombo replaced el Chino as a commander when the latter reported el Nato for secretly eating 'a whole fillet of meat', a betrayal Che felt el Chino should have stopped.

Camba had already requested to be allowed to leave the force and on September 13 a guerrilla named Darío did likewise. While others continued to express their full support and loyalty, the first cracks had appeared in the fabric of Che's company.

Despite all these factors (and despite his and the doctor's own appalling frailty), Che embarked on an exercise which seemed to break every fundamental rule of guerrilla warfare: moving his men in the open during the hours of daylight, moving through populated areas in which no support for them existed and the risk of betrayal was huge, displaying graphic evidence of the weakened state of his ragged little band as they limped (or were carried – in obvious distress – on mule-back) onwards, and not even retreating to the relative safety and cover of the jungle at night. On at least two occasions Che's desperate men simply set up camp on the side of the road, too tired – and in many ways too disorganized – to do the sensible thing.

That march took them through the villages of Lucitano, Alto Seco (where Inti gave a talk and the revolution 'to a group of 15 amazed and silent peasants' in the local primary school!), Santa Elena, Loma Larga (where Che's condition was worsened by a bout of vomiting), Pujio, Tranca Mayo, Picacho (in the midst of a fiesta) and, finally, Jagüey.

It was on the road to Jagüey that Che's advance party (he had remained in Picacho with the doctor and their last few mules) walked into an army ambush. Che quickly organized his group into defensive positions and tried to set plans for a retreat along a trail which led to the Grande river. After an agonizing wait, a wounded Benigno appeared, soon followed by Aniceto and Pablito, whose foot was 'in a bad mess'.

They confirmed that Miguel, Coco Peredo and Julio had been killed and Camba had simply dropped his rucksack and run away. As the rear party made for the Grande river trail under a hail of bullets from pursuing soldiers, Che realized that they had also lost contact with Inti and León, another Bolivian. Inti re-appeared, reporting that he'd seen León's rucksack abandoned in the defile through which he'd escaped.

With the army closing in on them from the rear, Che shooed the mules down one canyon while following his group into another. The trick worked and the guerrillas pushed on towards relative safety while the soldiers chased the mules, but it would not be until midnight that they could rest, their way blocked by high cliffs.

The task of finding a way out of the ravine began at 4 am and was not successful until three hours later, but as they laid low they saw a big army column on a nearby hill, while their preferred escape route was also cut off by a number of troops based in a nearby house. For three days they stayed hidden as various scouts returned to say that the whole area was alive with soldiers.

The radio told Che that he'd been in action against the Galindo company, that Camba and León remained at liberty, that the bodies of Miguel, Coco and Julio had been taken to Vallegrande for identification, that he himself was dead, then that he wasn't and, finally (in a Chilean broadcast), that he was now trapped in a wooded canyon.

At 10 pm on September 30, Che decided to head for the Grande river, about two kilometres away in a fairly straight line. Progress was slow, held up as they were by Benigno and el Chino's wounds and the continued decline in the doctor's condition.

Creeping and crawling their way through the rocky jungle terrain, on October 3 Che's radio brought news that León (Antonio Domínguez Flores) and Camba (Orlando Jiménez Bazán) had been captured. Worse, they were talking – about the make-up of his army, about Che's increasing sickness 'and all the rest, without counting what they must have said off the record. So ends the story of two heroic guerrilla fighters', Che noted wrily.

By October 7, with Chilean radio breaking Bolivian censorship to inform Che that there were now more than 1,800 troops involved in the hunt, he learned from an old woman goat-herder who wandered into the canyon where he and his 16 survivors were camped that they were 'about one league from Higueras and another from Jagüey, and about two from

Pucará.' In essence, they had put no real distance between the Bolivian military and themselves, despite seven gruelling days of severe privation, risk and constant danger.

The final entry in Che's diary concluded:

'At 17.30, Inti, Aniceto and Pablito went to the old woman's house, where she had one crippled and one dwarf daughter. She was given 50 pesos and charged with not speaking a word; we don't have much hope that she will keep her promises. The 17 of us went off under a small moon and the march was very tiresome and we left a lot of tracks in the canyon . . . At 02.00 we halted to rest, because it was useless to go on advancing. El Chino becomes a real burden when we have to travel by night.
'The army issued a strange report about the presence of 250 men in Serrano to stop the passage of the encircled men, who are said to number 37; they locate our hiding place between the Acero and Oro rivers.
'The news seems to be a red herring.'

It wasn't. Shortly after noon the next day, as Che and his guerrillas waited in the narrow Yuro Ravine for a much-needed rest until dark, when they planned to push on in an attempt to break through the cordon which encircled them, they were surprised by a large enemy force.

With some guerrillas on the ravine floor and others positioned on ledges higher up, and the guerrillas unable to see each other most of the time, the gunfight lasted for some hours. According to Fidel Castro, in his introduction to Che's Bolivian diary, there were to be 'no survivors among those who were fighting near Che'. Near him in the early stages of battle were the doctor and a Peruvian who was in poor condition, and while the doctor did survive this final showdown, he died some days later when some of the survivors – including Benigno, Pombo and Inti Peredo, who had managed to slip away from the enemy when dark fell – were ambushed once more.

Although wounded seriously in both legs, Che Guevara continued to fight until the barrel of his M-2 was destroyed by a bullet. The pistol he was carrying did not have a magazine so he was helpless to do anything as the Bolivian Rangers moved in to take him prisoner and carry his skinny, diseased and bullet-ridden figure to Higueras.

It was there that he died, and it was there that a legend was born. It is a legend which shows no sign of fading, even though new heroes come and go and the world moves on.

'I believe in armed struggle as the only solution for people who are fighting for freedom, and I act according to this belief. Many will call me an adventurer, and I am, but of a different kind – one who risks his skin to prove his convictions'

BACKGROUND The vanquished Che laid out for display by his victors.

The making of a Legend

Within weeks of Che's death, and while the horrific images of his corpse were still being run and re-run by print and broadcast media all around the world, it was clear that his murder (for that was precisely what US President Lyndon Johnson ordered when the CIA notified him of Che's capture and asked what message they should send to La Paz) had created both a martyr and a potent universal icon.

It was not merely that the famous Christ-like portrait of Che became one of the most popular images to appear on untold millions of posters which were sold as a *de riguer* decoration for the campus dorms, apartments and walk-up flats of politically aware youth; as is the way of the world, those same posters were destined – for a while, at least – to jostle for wall-space with pin-ups and pop idols in the bedrooms of teenagers who simply recognized a sexy hunk when they saw one.

Along with the posters came the myriad other merchandizing collectables the capitalist marketplace has always been able to produce at the sniff of a trend – T-shirts, buttons, badges, stickers and, on a more serious level, elegaic poems, paintings, musical tributes, as well as hundreds of books in as many languages, all of them attempting to tell The True Story even if much of the truth was destined to remain secret for as long as almost 30 years.

Many of those rushed-into-print volumes were brave and sincere attempts to pay fulsome homage to Che, his achievements and his beliefs. Most of them, however, suffered from a pious hero-worship Che himself would undoubtedly have found risible, for he knew that he was no saint, nor flawless, nor an undiluted hero.

Many more had a political agenda which rendered them all but unreadable to any but the few who had PhDs in political science or were able to wade through the dense, verbose semantics of Marxist-Trotskyist dogma with which they were packed. And far too many more were cut-and-paste jobs inevitably flawed by the inaccuracy or sloppiness of the original material they drew on for 'facts' and justly ended their days in the trash-can of publishing and political history.

It was only a matter of time before Hollywood tried to grab itself a piece of the lucrative action, and in 1969 screenwriter-turned-producer Sy Bartlett's *Che!* found its way onto the big screen. Starring Omar Sharif in the title role and Jack Palance as Fidel Castro, the exclamation mark in its title the only element of real excitement, *Che!* failed to deliver in spectacular fashion, with the possible exception of the make-up artists who transformed Omar Sharif into a reasonable facsimile of Guevara.

When, in 1976, lyricist Tim Rice and composer Andrew Lloyd Webber first devised the pop-opera *Evita*, they had no hesitation in opting for the figure of Che Guevara to act as an ironic observer-narrator of their version of the life, times and death of Eva Perón, the charismatic wife of the Argentine president whose dictatorial rule the real-life Che once took to the streets of Buenos Aires to vilify. *Evita* became one of the world's most successful and longest-running stage shows and eventually

BELOW A thoughtful Omar Sharif – looking remarkably like the real Che for Sy Bartlett's 1969 film, *Che!*

transferred to the big screen in 1996, when Madonna played the title role in a stylish production directed by Alan Parker. In that film Antonio Banderas delivered a passionate, sexy and flamboyant portrayal of Che to bring him to the attention of an even wider and even younger audience.

Already a hero and inspiration to aspiring revolutionaries long before his death – he was, remember a potent and ferociously charismatic figure who attracted huge crowds of adoring 'fans' when he toured the world – Che's own writings and speeches acquired a new potency and resonance with his death. They became required reading as far afield as London, Paris, Madrid, Rome, Prague, New York and Berkeley, California for the members of organizations as disparate as Britain's Angry Brigade, Germany's Red Army Faction/Baader-Meinhof Group, the Basque separatist movement, (ETA), Italy's Red Brigade, Nicaragua's Sandinistas and, in the US, the likes of The Weathermen and The Black Panthers.

For some time they remained resistant to the revision which the passing years and more objective reporting brought to the legend, even when Fidel Castro himself admitted to Che's flaws, carefully excusing them as inspired by a complete, overwhelming and selfless dedication to The Cause. Che's victories in the Cuban Revolutionary War were often due to his reckless, sometimes feckless impetuosity, but that was due, in turn, to his complete lack of self-regard. Victory was all that mattered, and if he died in battle, so what?

Disregard for one's own safety is one thing, but to demand that degree of fanaticism from those under your command is quite another. Che's inflexible response to any failure which he percieved as a lack of absolute commitment by any member of any regiment he led, was a supreme failure of his own humanity. And when that same inflexibility came into play as Che took on key governmental and political roles after the war, he became a loose cannon on the deck of the Cuban ship of state, itself already under heavy fire from its many enemies.

Such re-assessments of the Guevara legend were eventually bound to eat away at the foundations of the messainic idol the revolutionaries of

LEFT and RIGHT From the playground to the classroom, the image of Che is a part of life for the youth of Cuba.

the late 1960s and early 1970s had created for themselves. That, and the inevitable rise of new political tyros, the inevitable break-up of those original groups via death or imprisonment, and the pragmatic acceptance of mundane universal realities such as marriage, kids, mortgage payments and (whisper it) careers, meant that Che Guevara slipped down the ladder of political influence.

Down, but not off it altogether. Che Guevara continued – and still continues – to be a seminal figure in revolutionary circles. The Berlin Wall may have fallen, the Soviet Russian empire may have crumbled and the monolithic socialist states it sponsored may have turned themselves into desperate dollar-hungry tourist traps, but there are still many in whom the fire of revolution blazes and for whom the legend – and the life – of Che Guevara represents a shining example of what can be achieved with little more than a dream and the energy and force of will to make that dream become reality.

Not everyone shares the undiluted enthusiasm we are told we should all have for free market economics, unbridled capitalism and the like. There are victims out there. People still disappear in Argentina, in Brazil, Uruguay, Mexico, Burma and a host of other nations whose leaders and police chiefs deal with all and any opposition in the brutally effective fashion they know works supremely well.

There are still millions of casualties in scores of civil wars and avoidable famines. And there are still untold thousands of young radicals prepared to use insurrection and guerrilla warfare in addressing such offences against human rights.

For many of them, Che Guevara's clarion calls to arms remain, remarkably, as persuasive as ever, and he retains a dominant position in their canons of radical saints and visionaries, even if the object of their adulation has sometimes been revealed as all-too fallible, possessing all-too human feet of clay.

RIGHT The image of Che looks down on a political rally in the Plaza de la Revolucion, Havana 1983.

BELOW All over Cuba pictures of Che Guevara remind the people of their debt to this extraordinary man.

But it is the continued survival of Che Guevara as an icon of mid-century Western pop culture which is perhaps even more remarkable. Along with the likes of James Dean, Marilyn Monroe, Jim Morrison, Jimi Hendrix and John Lennon – all of them dead, and all of them dying relatively young – the immediately-recognisable stylised portrait of Che still adorns millions of T-shirts, and accounts for a healthy percentage of world poster sales.

And many such sales must be to people who were not only unborn when Che Guevara was making his mark on modern history, but who have only a very sketchy understanding of who and what he was, or what he stood for and did.

Modern visitors to Cuba – itself one of the nations still reeling from the economic ramifications of the Soviet Union's demise (and the United States' obdurate refusal to lift the punitive trade embargo it introduced in the early 1960s) and even now attempting to boost its international earnings via tourism – would expect to find ample evidence of Che Guevara's importance to that benighted island.

They are not, of course, disappointed. Street vendors and official tourist shops offer a wealth of Che merchandise, not all of it tasteful, much of it pure kitsch, and certainly enough to threaten the average traveller's baggage weight allowance on the way home if he or she bought up everything available.

Giant murals of Che still dominate major squares and highways in the capital and elsewhere. Memorials still proliferate in towns he helped liberate, while streets and plazas named after him are rivalled only by those dedicated to the likes of revolutionary Frank País (executed, along with captured members of the original Granma group, in 1956), Fidel Castro and the date July 26, when Castro's revolution began in earnest.

If all that is no less than you would expect, its is worth noting that secondary school pupils in Bolivia are still, even now, obliged to study Che Guevara as part of their country's core curriculum, while the rest of South America contains many memorials to the man who once dreamed of making the entire continent a socialist Utopia. Few, of course, were erected by the governments of those countries but by men and women who shared – and still pursue – that dream.

Che's continued importance – and the universality of the fascination he still exerts on the public's imagination thirty years after his death – is perhaps best illustrated by the fact that, as this book was being completed, a cursory trawl of the Internet revealed no less than seven thousand web-sites including his name as a key reference, in scores of languages. It was fair to assume that number would only increase as the anniversary of his murder grew ever nearer.

Barely a year passes when new books about Che are not published somewhere in the world. It is also fair to assume that this particular offering will be only one of many more published, long after the 30th anniversary of his death in October 1997.

Che Guevara may be dead, but he is still a potent symbol for the world's dispossessed and disenchanted, its radicals and revolutionaries, and for those who remain intrigued by a man who was prepared to pay the ultimate price for his pursuit of an unselfish vision of a brighter future.

RIGHT The most famous Guevara image that has been used the world over evolved from this picture by photographer Alberto Korda, which was itself a cropped version of a wider shot that included another person on the left of the picture.

'Because of the circumstances in which I travelled, first as a student and later as a doctor, I came into close contact with poverty, hunger, and disease; with the inability to treat a child because of lack of money; with the stupefaction provoked by continual hunger and punishment, to the point that a father can accept the loss of a son as an unimportant accident . . . and I began to realize that there were things which were almost as important to me as becoming a famous scientist or making a significant contribution to medical science: I wanted to help those people.'

‘Our sacrifice is a conscious one:
it is in payment for the freedom
we are building.’

First published in 1997 by Hamlyn, an imprint of
Octopus Publishing Group Ltd.

This 2001 edition published by Chancellor Press,
an imprint of Bounty Books, a division of
Octopus Publishing Group Ltd,
2-4 Heron Quays, London E14 4JP

Printed and bound in Hong Kong

Publishing Director: Laura Bamford
Executive Editor: Mike Evans
Editor: Humaira Husain
Art Director: Keith Martin
Senior Designer: Geoff Borin
Production Controller: Dawn Mitchell
Picture Research: Maria Gibbs

Acknowledgements

The author wishes to acknowledge the following sources:

Bolivian Diary Ernesto Che Guevara (Jonathan Cape / Lorrimer,
London 1968)
Che Guevara Jean Cormier (with Hilda Guevara & Alberto Granado)
(Editions Gallimard, Paris 1995)
**The Motorcycle Diaries: A Journey Around South
America** Ernesto Che Guevara, translated by Ann Wright
(Fourth Estate, London 1996)
**Venceremos! The Speeches and Writings of
Che Guevara** Edited by John Gerassi (Weidenfeld & Nicolson,
London 1968)
Episodes of the Cuban Revolutionary War
Ernesto Che Guevara, edited by Mary-Alice Waters (Pathfinder Press,
New York 1996)
Che Guevara and the Congo Richard Gott (New Left Review,
London 1997)
Congo Mercenary Mike Hoare (publisher not known, London 1967)
Loués soient nos seigneurs: une éducation politique
Régis Debray (Editions Gallimard, Paris 1995)

Picture Credits